FLY FISHING IDAHO'S SECRET WATERS

CHRIS HUNT

Published by The History Press
Charleston, SC 29403
www.historypress.net

Copyright © 2014 by Chris Hunt
All rights reserved

All photos courtesy of the author unless otherwise noted.

First published 2014

Manufactured in the United States

ISBN 978.1.62619.216.4

Library of Congress Cataloging-in-Publication Data

Hunt, Chris, 1969-
Fly fishing Idaho's secret waters / Chris Hunt.
pages. cm
ISBN 978-1-62619-216-4
1. Fly fishing--Idaho I. Title.
SH487.H86 2014
799.12'409796--dc23
2014001911

Notice: The information in this book is true and complete to the best of our knowledge. It is offered without guarantee on the part of the author or The History Press. The author and The History Press disclaim all liability in connection with the use of this book.

All rights reserved. No part of this book may be reproduced or transmitted in any form whatsoever without prior written permission from the publisher except in the case of brief quotations embodied in critical articles and reviews.

CONTENTS

Foreword 7
Acknowledgements 11
Introduction 13

1. Past and Present 21
2. Secret Idaho 31
3. Eastern Idaho 41
4. Southern Idaho 65
5. Central Idaho 85
6. Northern Idaho 107

About the Author 127

FOREWORD

Fly fishing in the backcountry is like playing acoustic music. It's raw, honest, essential.

Minus the augmentation, amplification, overdubs and such, it's pretty clear who can really carry a tune and who cannot, who knows how to harmonize and improvise beyond the fundamentals and who simply reads sheet music and depends on engineers (like fly-fishing guides) to make them sound good.

It's exactly the same when you pick up a fly rod. So many of the "nice fish, pretty colors" photos we see in books and magazines these days are taken on "prolific trout factory" waters, and usually that involves a tailwater fishery on a well-worn path near a highway parking lot. It often revolves around playing "bobber ball" with a strike indicator and tiny nymph flies, wherein anglers hope to squeeze one more timid take out of fish that have been literally flogged into submission.

To me, at least, the true essence of this sport is rooted in exploration. I like to watch trout eat dry flies—not necessarily because I like the real-time visual stimulus but because I've come to learn that in the right place, at the right time, that's exactly what trout naturally want to do.

Being willing to walk (or drive) the hard miles to find these fish and then cast in the tiny (sometimes anonymous) blue lines on a topographic map is the key to discovering the true riches this sport has to offer. When you really pull that off, you never, ever forget why you fell in love with fly fishing in the first place.

Chris Hunt is my favorite "acoustic" artist when it comes to fly fishing. He has a knack for landing on the essence. Mind you, there have been times when I have openly wondered about playing along with him.

For example, he once invited me to chase native cutthroats in remote canyon drainages for a week, which I was more than eager to do. On day one, he said, "We're just going to drop down into the river here," which we did. It seemed like the right thing to do at the time, and indeed we caught many native fish. But climbing out at the end of the day in sandals and shorts—scaling eight hundred vertical feet through a field of scree, panting and wheezing—I had to ask aloud, "Dude—is every day going to be like this?"

I shouldn't have asked. But, aw heck, it was worth it. I became a better man—and a better angler—for having done so. In subsequent years, Chris has continued to show me hidden-jewel fishing spots that inevitably make me a better fisherman. The guy has a lot of aces up his sleeve, especially when it comes to Idaho.

Which leads me to a sensitive subject and one I think we should get out on the table right now. Idaho is the "Gem State," after all, and when we get into the business of talking about hidden gems, at least in the context of fishing, well, is spilling the beans really a good thing to do?

For those who wonder, I have a two-word response: get real.

Idaho is the seventh-least populated of the fifty states. It's easily one of the top ten fly-fishing destinations in the world. There's more than enough to go around. It's only natural, therefore—actually, it's essential—to scratch beyond the surface and inspire people to explore and understand what the state really has to offer. I am grateful that Chris has done so, and in a way that I have never seen before.

The truth is that I'm writing this in a notebook on the banks of Lago Quiroga, in Santa Cruz province, in southern Argentina. I am here

Foreword

chasing a magazine story that will no doubt revolve around the massive rainbow trout to be found here.

But in all honesty—even now, even here—my heart and soul are inextricably connected to the backcountry in the American West.

You see, the more you venture and the more you experience, the more you realize that there is indeed "no place like home," and you understand that the greatest, wildest, most exciting fly-fishing adventures don't really start with a travel brochure, an international plane ticket or some faraway lodge.

The best ones always start with your own feet. And if you're willing to walk to discover the hidden gems, fishing-wise, you'll find fulfillment and excitement that lasts a lifetime. In fact, there's so much out there that one lifetime is surely not enough to allow any angler to experience it all.

This book shortens the learning curve and puts you on the right path. The hours and insights here speak volumes. The honesty is admirable. The prose is eloquent. The purpose is genuine. The substance is hard-earned. And the opportunities, well, they speak for themselves.

So read on. Play along. And then compose your own acoustic music. Fish the "unplugged" rivers. You'll be glad you did.

Kirk Deeter
Editor, *TROUT* magazine

ACKNOWLEDGEMENTS

To my friend Scott Stouder for showing me what the backcountry is truly all about, and to my dear friend Rachel Morgan, who's never afraid to explore. To my buddy Tom Reed, who understands what blue lines are really all about. To Kirk Deeter, for whom friendship is a serious and unfailing proposition. And to my children, Delaney and Cameron, for reminding me why protecting the places I love is so important.

INTRODUCTION

They call this a "cold front." It's eighty-two degrees and raining sideways. The emerald waters of Florida Bay are chalky and rough. It's muggy. Everything in my travel bag smells like…feet.

It's been eight days since I left Idaho, and I'm ready to go home.

To appreciate home, sometimes you have to leave for a while. To value something is to miss it when it's gone. Or when you're gone. Simple as that.

As I sit here in a musty hotel room on Key Largo, I am wishing the heavy eight-weight leaning against the wall was a supple, fiberglass three-weight and that the water outside wasn't salty and violent but cold and clear and a mile away from the road. I wish the slate-gray sky was astonishingly blue and that the pelicans that loitered at the docks were instead ospreys scolding me as I cast a fat foam hopper to a beefy cutthroat they marked from one hundred feet above.

I wish, at this moment, that I were back home in Idaho where I belong.

The Gem State harbors many fishy secrets, from little-known tailwaters where rotund brown trout chase streamers every day of the year to small, hidden Panhandle creeks where redbands and westslope cutthroats feed on mayflies while keeping a wary eye on the depths, knowing a two-foot-long bull trout could be eyeing them for a meal.

Introduction

It's a diverse state. The Owyhees are a canyon-lover's delight and harbor backcountry secrets known only to a few. In the middle of the state flows the Salmon River, the "River of No Return"—to this day, it runs unimpeded on its journey from its headwaters atop Galena Summit to its confluence with the mighty Snake near Hell's Canyon. Just a bit farther south flow the Big Wood and the fabled waters of Hemingway's Silver Creek, a big-fish destination that has confounded some of the best fly fishers on earth for the better part of a century.

From the east flow the headwaters of the Snake—Henry's Fork and the South Fork. Henry's Fork bubbles up from the ground at Big Springs, just west of the Yellowstone National Park boundary, and flows south, slicing through the Island Park Caldera until it spills over Mesa Falls and then courses down the Snake River Plain. It meets the South Fork, which essentially gets its start in the Yellowstone backcountry before flowing through Grand Teton National Park and the Snake River Canyon in western Wyoming. As it leaves the bottom of Palisades Reservoir, the river takes on its South Fork name—and adopts the reputation as perhaps the best dry-fly destination fishery in America—and flows through Swan Valley and Conant Valley.

The two rivers meet at Menan, forming the Snake once again. This mighty river bisects the Snake River Plain, a swath of flat, volcanic prairie land stretching from one side of southern Idaho to the next. As it flows, it loses its "trouty" character and becomes, in some stretches, a

Above: A caddis fly touches down on a patch of snow and ice along Henry's Fork.

Right: The author casts for redbands in a remote Owyhee canyon in southern Idaho. *Photo by Rachel Morgan.*

Following pages: The author wanders up a lonely, unnamed creek in the Owyhees. Sometimes they're fishy... sometimes they're not.

Introduction

Liza Raley fishes the Warm River in January.

quality smallmouth bass river. For a few renegade fly-rodders, however, the Snake holds a population of the strongest freshwater fish—pound for pound—found in the country. It's a carp-lover's paradise, where casts across flats rival those found in much more elegant destinations, where the targets themselves are more elegant as well.

It's easy to envision this amazing place when holed up in a south Florida hotel room while a squall blows across the Gulf of Mexico. But it's even better, with your boots on the ground, to experience Idaho with a fly rod in hand, a trail or a lonely gravel road stretched out before you and the promise of a hopper hatch looming.

It's even worth it to find some unheralded blue line in the *Gazetteer* and just start wandering. Sometimes these little creeks are fishy; sometimes they're not. But they never disappoint.

Introduction

I suppose it's easy to yearn for a cold, clear backcountry stream—I do my share of yearning during Idaho's brutal winters and, apparently, while I wait out a storm in the Keys. Those perfect days spent casting to rising trout far away from the nearest stretch of pavement burn images on my brain that are difficult to replicate in reality, but they come through easily enough when the world outside is a bit frightful.

When the snow blows sideways and that thermometer dips below zero, I know that I'm repaying Idaho for its bounty it delivers much of the rest of the year. And I know that, during a thaw in February, I'll brave the elements and wander to the river. I'll bundle up in Neoprene and utter phrases like, "I'm too old for this shit" or "What on earth was I thinking?" But then the line will tighten and a feisty trout will dash off into the current, and I'll know that, for the hearty angler, Idaho's hoard of fishy water can be tapped at virtually any time.

But Idaho can't be accessed from the steamy environs of the Florida Keys, at least not directly. I've found a way, though, to tap my Idaho from afar. As the rain beats against the window, I know that somewhere at home, a fat brown is chasing a streamer under that perfect October sky to the delight of a fly fisher with enough common sense to stay home. I'm not that angler. Not this year.

But I will be for years to come.

Chris Hunt
Key Largo, Florida
October 19, 2013

Chapter 1
PAST AND PRESENT

*I*daho may not be a breadbasket of fly fishing history like, say, the Catskills. And it might not enjoy the well-earned reputation of Montana or the romance of the Caribbean flats. But Idaho is a vast, fishy wonderland that, for generations, has lured anglers to its waters.

Comparatively, however, it remains largely untapped as a fly-fishing destination, at least compared to the more storied places like Patagonia, New Zealand, Alaska and, yes, neighboring Montana.

That said, fabled waters like Henry's Fork or Silver Creek draw anglers from every corner of the globe—these are waters of legend. Ernest Hemingway was an avid Silver Creek angler, but truthfully, most of his fishing was done in the salty environs of the Florida Keys or farther south in Cuba. Instead, he loved Silver Creek for the duck hunting, a passion he acquired after staying in the Big Wood River Valley compliments of the Sun Valley Resort. It was customary for the resort to provide lodging for celebrities like Hemingway and the Hollywood glitter crowd of the 1930s, including Gary Cooper, Greta Garbo and Errol Flynn.

However, Hemingway's son, Jack, dearly loved to fly fish, and today, Silver Creek Preserve is in the hands of the Nature Conservancy largely because Jack, from his position on the Idaho Fish and Game Commission,

Michelle Bryant of Twin Falls, Idaho, wades the sacred waters of Silver Creek.

helped negotiate the purchase of much of Silver Creek when the Sun Valley Ranch put its holdings up for sale in the 1970s.

Hemingway might have been Idaho's most well-known citizen, albeit a part-time resident at best. Sadly, Idaho is where he chose to take his own life after slipping into failing health. He died on July 2, 1961. His legacy

Past and Present

lives on, however. Two memorials mark his time in the Gem State: one on Trail Creek above the Sun Valley Resort and another on the banks of Silver Creek, where he hunted and occasionally fished. The Sun Valley Heritage and Ski Museum boasts a Hemingway exhibit that covers in great detail "Papa's" time in the area.

While Hemingway might be Idaho's most famous resident, Idaho's favorite son, particularly when it comes to hunting and fishing, is no doubt Ted Trueblood. The renowned outdoor writer called Idaho home his entire life, even after stints living in New York and Salt Lake City, where he worked for *Field & Stream* and the *Deseret News*, respectively. Trueblood communicated about Idaho better than any other writer—ever—and his tales of fishing and hunting in Idaho are legendary.

Trueblood's true legacy, though, lies in conservation. Idaho boasts the largest swath of undeveloped backcountry in the Lower 48, largely because Trueblood helped stop the construction of the Nez Perce Dam on the Snake River in the 1950s, which would have halted the migration of salmon and steelhead up the Salmon River. To this day, despite the eventual construction of five dams on the lower Snake River in Washington, thousands of salmon and steelhead make their way into the Salmon River and run as far as the Sawtooth Fish Hatchery above the

A memorial to Ernest Hemingway rests on the banks of Silver Creek.

town of Stanley. That's about nine hundred miles from the salty estuary where the Columbia River meets the Pacific.

The Salmon River remains undammed, and in the summer, it's perhaps the best wilderness float trip an angler can take—willing westslope cutthroat trout hit dry flies as the river flows through the Frank Church River of No Return Wilderness. In the fall, it's home to a legendary run of "B-run" steelhead—massive oceangoing rainbow trout that can push thirty inches and twenty pounds. Not coincidentally, it was the sportsman and outdoor writer Ted Trueblood who advocated for the creation of that wilderness in the 1970s in the face of the anti-federal "Sagebrush Rebellion" that swept across the West. But Trueblood, it could be argued, was much more Western than the foam-at-the-mouth crowd that orchestrated the anti-environmental movement. He hunted and fished, and he understood that without intact habitats, clean water and connected landscapes, the hunting and fishing that were (and still are) a treasured part of the Western heritage would fade away. The wilderness was officially designated in 1980.

Sadly, not unlike Hemingway, Trueblood fell ill and took his own life in 1982. He was sixty-nine years old. Much of Trueblood's work can be found in a special collection at Boise State University. Today, the Trout Unlimited chapter in Boise bears his name.

Other names prominent in fly-fishing history have deep ties to Idaho, and to the Henry's Fork in particular. Legendary fly fisherman Bing Lempke grew up in Idaho Falls and started fly fishing in 1926. Over the years, he became known for his extended body flies that matched Henry's Fork famous green drake hatch, one of the more storied hatches on American waters.

Another fly invented on the banks of Henry's Fork was created by the former mayor of Chicago, Carter H. Harrison. Legend has it that in September 1901, Harrison was a guest at a ranch owned by A.S. Trude. While staying at the ranch and engaging in some friendly banter, Harrison took a massive hook he used as a gaff for muskies in the upper Midwest and fashioned a fly with it. He noticed a red spaniel lying on the floor, and he clipped a few hairs from the dog. Then, he clipped some red yarn from the ranch's rug and spun it on the massive hook. He then presented the "fly" to Mr. Trude as a jocular thanks for his hospitality—it likely can't be confirmed, but it's probable that more than a few cocktails were consumed in the hours leading up this invention.

Harrison, presumably after sobering up, took a good, long look at the prank fly and decided it could be fashioned into something usable on a smaller hook. He tied two flies on size-four hooks—one with red yarn wrapped with silver tinsel and the other identical to it but tied with green yard instead. Red squirrel hair was used instead of the dog hair for the wing, and red rooster hackle was wrapped ahead of the wing. He and a friend fished the fly the next day on the Buffalo River, a tributary to Henry's Fork. Harrison and his friend filled two creels with big cutthroat trout and presented the bounty to Mr. Trude that evening.

Rachel Morgan of Boise, Idaho, fishes a wilderness tributary to the Salmon River.

Today, the fly is known as the Trude, and there are dozens of variants of this initial pattern that worked so well, including the famous Rio Grande King. Unfortunately, the Yellowstone cutthroats that once coursed through the water of Henry's Fork and its tributaries are all but gone, replaced by nonnative rainbows and browns. Native whitefish still come to hand frequently, a reminder that Henry's Fork is still healthy and productive, even if the fish swimming in it don't necessarily belong there.

Today, Idaho fly fishing is a culture in and of itself. From legendary fly shops like Jimmy's All-Seasons Angler in Idaho Falls to the colorful guides and outfitters who wander the storied rivers like Henry's Fork and the South Fork, Idaho has become a low-key mecca for anglers.

World-renowned anglers like Mike Lawson and Rene Harrop still rub elbows with everyday fly fishers who come on pilgrimages to the fabled Railroad Ranch in Island Park. "The Ranch," as it's called in virtually every publication that's ever run an article on Henry's Fork, is a stretch of the famous river running through what was once part of a working cattle ranch owned by the Harriman and Guggenheim families. Averell Harriman, who made his fortune as the owner of the Union Pacific Railroad, deeded the ranch to the state of Idaho in 1977. It opened to the public in 1982, and Henry's Fork has become a bucket-list staple ever since.

The Ranch has been romanced by some of the best fly-fishing writers ever, including Ernie Schweibert, Gary LaFontaine and John Gierach.

The South Fork of the Snake is perhaps the best-kept secret in American fly fishing. Home to one of the last big-water populations of Yellowstone cutthroat trout within its native range, this river's reputation as a dry-fly fishery is well deserved. But during the fall spawn, it's also one of the best rivers in the country to hook into big brown trout on streamers, and it's also home to rainbow trout and native mountain whitefish. It's a favorite destination for the likes of former vice president Dick Cheney and a lot of the big-money crowd from nearby Jackson Hole, Wyoming.

Farther north along the Montana border flows Kelly Creek, one of the West's best cutthroat trout streams. But it's the human history along this creek that is most fascinating. Lee Sappington, an archaeology professor at the University of Idaho, is leading an archaeological dig investigating

Above: Rachel Morgan fishes Rainey Creek, a tributary of the South Fork in eastern Idaho.

Opposite: A Henry's Fork rainbow trout.

some of the earliest known human inhabitants of Idaho. Finds in recent years indicate that human inhabitants were present in the area along Kelly Creek two thousand years earlier than previously believed, and some of the implements found—like spear points fashioned from lava rock not found in the area—suggest that the Nez Perce tribe of northern Idaho likely traded with the Indian tribes of southern Idaho, southern Oregon and Montana. The find along Kelly Creek is significant, as the stream was once connected to the Columbia River system. (Dworshak Dam on the North Fork of the Clearwater was completed in 1973, cutting off access to Kelly Creek for salmon and steelhead migrating up from the Pacific.) Kelly Creek is a fly rodder's paradise, and it flows through some of the best intact trout and char habitat in the West. That it was likely used as a fishery by the Nez Perce tribe thousands of years ago makes it a storied water no less significant than the Henry's Fork or the South Fork of the Snake.

Chapter 2
SECRET IDAHO

I remain hopeful that I will be able to pass on to my grandchildren all the pleasures of life in an unspoiled West. Perhaps hope should be replaced by a stronger word. It is a matter of obligation.
—*Cecil Andrus, former governor of Idaho and former Secretary of the Interior*

In the mid-2000s, anglers and hunters in Idaho took a leading role in protecting the state's last untracked wild lands. Idaho is blessed with about 9 million acres of "roadless" land within the U.S. Forest Service system in the state, and thanks largely to sportsmen like Scott Stouder of Riggins, most of that backcountry habitat will remain protected for generations to come.

In 2005, President Bush replaced the 2001 Roadless Rule put in place at the tail end of the Clinton administration. That first rule offered blanket protection for some 58 million acres of "roadless" land all throughout the country. The Bush Rule offered states the chance to manage that land according to a customized set of rules, and Idaho was one of only two states that jumped at the chance to determine how land within its borders were to be managed.

The Tetons loom over a field of wildflowers in the Warm River drainage of eastern Idaho.

Following pages: Scott Stouder fishes the Clearwater River backcountry. *Photo by Greg McReynolds.*

Stouder, who works for Trout Unlimited as a sportsman organizer, worked closely with then-governor Jim Risch and a collaborative group representing all sorts of interest groups to identify the best of the best in the state and determine varying levels of protection for land based on their backcountry qualities. Risch was eventually elected to the U.S. Senate in 2006, and he continued to shepherd the Idaho rule through to completion. In 2008, the Idaho-specific roadless rule was put into place, and the vast majority of the state's backcountry lands were protected, both for the fish and game that call these lands home and for the people who use them for recreation.

Sportsmen are the most obvious beneficiaries of this rule—much of Idaho is a wild paradise and will remain so for generations, thanks to the collaborative approach to backcountry land management.

During the process, Stouder was able to identify not only the lands that had the highest value but also how much Idaho's native fish depended on waters flowing through or from roadless lands in the state. He learned that 68 percent of the state's native—and endangered—bull trout population swims in waters within roadless

backcountry areas. Anadromous fish—salmon and steelhead that return to Idaho to spawn after swimming about eight hundred miles from the ocean—depend even more on Idaho's backcountry fisheries. According to a TU report compiled by Stouder in 2004, 74 percent of Idaho's returning salmon and steelhead spawn in waters within inventoried roadless areas. And 58 percent of the state's westslope cutthroat trout live in backcountry waters.

For the angler, this data is golden. From a conservation perspective, it's a no-brainer—protecting the backcountry protects our fish. But let's take this a step further—protecting the backcountry protects our fishing. Habitat and opportunity go hand-in-hand in Idaho and anywhere else anglers chase fish of any species.

But that opportunity also translates into economic activity. In Idaho alone, fishing is a significant economic driver, contributing $756 million in 2011 to the state's economy. According to the American Sportfishing Association, there were more than 5.5 million "angler days" spent on the water that year, and the state raised nearly $50 million in tax revenue on the backs of anglers. In 2011, fishing supported 7,200 jobs in Idaho and provided almost $230 million in wages.

But enough about the data, as compelling as it is. Instead, consider the fishy bounty contained within the Idaho backcountry—the trout and char that might see only a few flies (or none) over the course of a fishing season. Imagine the beauty and the untracked, un-trashed places where wild fish swim.

This is the secret Idaho. And it's yours. All 9 million acres of it on U.S. Forest Service land and millions more found on Bureau of Land Management property belong to every single American as a birthright. It could be easily argued that protecting it in perpetuity is in the best interest of every angler willing to step off the pavement in Idaho and explore a little bit. I certainly believe that to be true.

When I set out to write this book, I heard a lot of people gasp at the notion of sharing "secret waters" with anyone willing to drop a few bucks at Amazon. Secret fishing spots, they said, are paid for in shoe leather and cold January nights spent combing over the *Gazetteer*. Secret waters

Liza Raley fishes Birch Creek, one of the "sink" streams of southern Idaho.

are proprietary, I was told. If people want to discover great backcountry fishing, let them pour over maps on their own.

Hogwash.

There's so much water in Idaho that the waters I'll describe in this book will truly amount to giving anglers a short head start on their own journey to discover backcountry treasures filled with wild fish and experiences we all thrive to uncover. What's more, our backcountry and our backcountry trout deserve the appreciation of anglers who, without a bit of encouragement, might not venture very far from the blacktop to chase fish. The more anglers who experience the backcountry, the more allies our wild fish have when it comes time to beat back a bad idea or stand up to those who don't share our conservation values. Anglers—and hunters—are more and more important in the conservation discussion

DeLorme's *Idaho Atlas & Gazetteer* is a must for any angler hoping to uncover Idaho's fishing secrets.

all across America. If this book encourages one angler to wander down a lonely trail and marvel at the wallpaper along a backcountry stream, it's worth it. If it gives one angler the motivation to write a letter to Congress or craft a letter to the editor of his local paper when that action is needed to protect the backcountry and our Idaho way of life, it's worth it.

Secrets? Sure, there are a few. But the real secrets of Idaho are still out there, awaiting the wandering fisher who, armed with a three-weight and a box of dry flies, can literally step back in time and experience the best of Idaho.

But perhaps to satisfy any potential critics—or at least to partially salve their concerns—I've refrained from offering specific instructions to the places I'll describe in the pages to come. Rather, I've simply offered general directions and the relevant page number(s) in DeLorme's *Idaho Atlas & Gazetteer*. Certainly a little map won't hurt the average angler—in fact, my hope is that it will inspire anglers to find blue lines on the map that I haven't mentioned. These, of course, are the real secret waters of Idaho.

There are a lot of fishable streams out there. Enjoy this head start—or, as my son would say, the "cheat code." I think you'll find it valuable, but I hope rather than just fishing the places I'll describe in the pages to come, you'll be inspired to wander up lonely trails along those blue lines on the map. If you do this, you'll find something much more valuable than secret fishing holes—you'll find the Idaho I adore. I think you'll come to love it, too.

Chapter 3

EASTERN IDAHO

*E*astern Idaho, from a fly fisher's perspective, is defined by the hallowed waters of Henry's Fork and the South Fork. But other rivers in the area are worthy of mention—and certainly worthy of fishing. Eastern Idaho is home to waters like the Bear River, which actually starts in the High Uintas of northeast Utah, flows into Wyoming and then eventually into the southeast corner of Idaho, where it takes a hard left and flows east through the Mormon settlement towns of Montpelier and Grace. It then takes another abrupt left and flows south, where it eventually dumps into the Great Salt Lake.

The Bear River drainage is home to Idaho's only population of Bonneville cutthroat trout, perhaps the heartiest of the cutthroat subspecies. These fish thrive in water that can reach temperatures considered unbearable for "tougher" brown trout. My friend Warren Colyer, a biologist and the director of Trout Unlimited's Western Conservation Program, studied the Bear River's cutthroats and found them to be highly migratory. They push into the tributaries of the Bear beneath the cover of spring runoff and swim dozens and dozens of miles into the cold, snowmelt-swollen creeks, where they spawn as early as May and into June. By July, just as the waters are receding, these big migratory natives—some as big as

Greg McReynolds fishes the Buffalo River, a tributary to Henry's Fork in eastern Idaho.

Salmon River steelhead—are back in the soupy waters of the Bear River, feeding on chubs and baby carp in water hardly considered trouty.

Then there's the Portneuf River, a once-fabled spring creek that flows south from the Shoshone-Bannock Indian Reservation through the little resort town of Lava Hot Springs and eventually through Pocatello. It meets the Snake River as it flows into American Falls Reservoir. The Portneuf's native fish is the Yellowstone cutthroat trout, but the river is also home to browns, rainbows and the now-frequent rainbow-cutthroat hybrid.

Years ago, the upper Portneuf—the cherished stretch of river that once held fishing comparable to that found in Henry's Fork—was drastically impacted by overgrazing. Cattle wallowed in the river's once-clear waters, widening its banks and making it hospitable to invasive species such as the common carp. In the 1980s— and continuing today—the Southeast Idaho Fly Fishers Chapter of Trout Unlimited began to work with the King Creek Grazing Association to funnel cows to hard-pan watering areas on the river, and as a result, habitat in the Portneuf continues to get better and better. Not coincidentally, so does the fishing.

And, of course, there's the Blackfoot River. Idaho's version is smaller than Montana's offering, but it can be no less fishy. Home to a run of native Yellowstone cutthroat trout that migrate out of Blackfoot Reservoir and into the river's upper reaches, the Blackfoot is the quintessential meadow stream, with deep overhanging banks and lots of cover for migrating cutthroats.

Much like the nearby Portneuf River, the Blackfoot suffered from development, both agricultural and, for generations now, phosphate mining that contributes selenium pollution to the watershed.

Efforts are underway to restore the Blackfoot and its tributaries to their former glory, and it's possible that the already good fishing found today on the well-known Stocking Ranch could be replicated throughout the system.

Finally, there's the Teton River, which is probably best known for the flood that ripped through the upper Snake River Valley in 1976. As the ill-advised Teton Dam was being filled for the first time on the morning of June 5, 1976, the earth structure began to leak. By noon, the dam had given way, sending about 2 million cubic feet of water down the Teton River canyon and eventually out onto the Snake River Plain. The massive flood all but destroyed the town of Sugar City, and Rexburg sustained serious damage as well. In all, fourteen people died in the flood.

Today, the river has largely recovered from the catastrophe, as have the communities located along it. And fishing on the Teton, home to native Yellowstone cutthroat trout, might be better today than it has been in generations. The Teton Canyon stretch is a favorite backcountry float among the guiding community, but accessing it is tough and requires that pontoon crafts be lowered to the water using ropes. The fishing for dry-fly-loving cutthroats, though, makes the effort worthwhile.

But these are all big waters.

The region is pretty vast. In fifteen years of living in eastern Idaho, I've only scratched the surface when it comes to fishable water. And, yes, the big-name rivers are truly magical—I'd put this corner of

Idaho up against some of the more storied fly-fishing destinations in the West any day. And while the collection of big water is astounding, it's the backcountry fishing in this corner of Idaho that goes almost completely unnoticed.

From beefy native cutthroats in small water to spunky brookies in tiny spring creeks atop the Island Park caldera, anglers could spend a lifetime traveling gravel roads and walking hidden trails and still not hit every fishable creek in the area.

Moose Creek

It looks like one of those places where something big and hairy could appear at just about any time. The little spring creek that flows through a long-burned-over stand of lodgepoles meanders through a meadow that just screams, "Bear!" There's lots of forage in the summer, including balsamroot—a gorgeous yellow wildflower that both black and grizzly bears love to eat. I once watched a large black bear mow through an entire field of these flowers in about an hour near the petrified tree access road in Yellowstone National Park.

And while this little creek isn't in the park, all the critters that roam Yellowstone can be found here.

So, as I floated a fluffy Adams over each deep pocket of Moose Creek and along every fishy cut bank, the itch in the back of my brain remained. Something was going to happen—I just knew it.

Years ago, before nonnative fish like brook trout and rainbows were transported across the country to Idaho, Moose Creek was likely a pretty lively Yellowstone cutthroat trout stream. Well-meaning fisheries

The skeletons of lodgepole pines burned decades ago loom over Moose Creek in eastern Idaho.

managers introduced brookies to the area over century ago, and while they didn't take hold in the big-water habitat of Henry's Fork—to which Moose Creek is a tributary—they're doing just fine in some of the smaller tributaries.

Brookies are native to the upper Midwest and Appalachia, and they require the coldest, cleanest water to survive and thrive. They possess, in my humble opinion, the zestiest life force of any trout or char in America, and this is the reason they do very well in small, austere waters. They do so well, in fact, that in many cases, they outgrow their environment and eventually stunt, becoming a large population of very small fish.

While the brook trout in Moose Creek certainly don't get awfully big, they're respectable. Most are in the six- to eight-inch range, but there are bigger fish that will stretch a tape one foot or longer. One of the largest brook trout I ever caught—fifteen inches—came from Moose Creek late one June evening that I remember more for the swarms of mosquitoes that descended on me like a miniature flight of Russian MIGs than I do for the fishing.

That is, until the big brookie hit the Royal Coachman I was using and then dove beneath a cut bank.

But on this day, the fishing was predictably solid—not spectacular. Moose Creek is so clear that it's easy to spook it's resident char, and it needs to be fished strategically in order to be fished successfully. If you're a dry-fly junky, Moose Creek will present some challenges. You'll need to be able to perform long casts with light tippets, and flies will need to be presented lightly and on target.

The flavor of fly is not terribly important—the waters of Moose Creek are so pristine that its insect life, while present, is pretty sparse. Anything that looks like food will get a look, but the presentation has to be spot on, and you'll need to keep low profile.

Greg McReynolds fishes Moose Creek in the Island Park Caldera of eastern Idaho.

A brook trout shows off its colors in the Buffalo River of eastern Idaho.

When I fish Moose Creek—and I make a point to do so at least once each summer—I do a lot of casting from my knees along the grassy banks, or, in certain spots, I'll cast over twenty feet of grass to the water just to keep from getting too close.

The rewards are many, however. Moose Creek's brookies are brilliantly marked, and there's a chance—albeit a small one—that you'll coax a smallish rainbow from the uber-clear waters as well.

On this occasion, as I fished upstream on a smoky summer day (Idaho's fire season was well under way), I was on high alert. For some reason, I felt like I was being watched, and as I looked around the meadow and through the sparse young lodgepoles, I expected to make eye contact with a bear.

As I rounded a fishy bend on the creek, I heard something rustle in the woods behind me. I turned quickly, my hand reaching to my hip for a can of bear spray that wasn't there (I'd managed to leave it in the truck in my haste to get to the water). Then I noticed something big—very big—ranging through the trees. Brown and beastly, I expected a grizzly to push through the young pines and glare at me from the water's edge. Instead, a massive cow moose stepped from the greenery and stopped not forty feet from where I stood. How appropriate, given my location.

My heart slowed and lowered back into my chest cavity from the awkward place in my throat. While moose can be a bit moody, they're generally docile, especially if you don't get too close or behave too carelessly. I snapped a couple of photos of my new friend and went back to chasing brookies, relieved to know that I wasn't being hunted by a massive bruin but rather simply investigated by a curious ungulate.

A cow moose inspects an angler along eastern Idaho's Moose Creek.

Flies

As I said, Moose Creek's brook trout aren't really picky when it comes to flies. They're more wary and spooky, so as long as the presentation is solid and the tippet is in the 5X range, you can get away with a fly that actually suits you more than it does the fish. Early in the year, I almost always go with a caddis or a Stimulator to mimic the caddis hatches on the water and the golden stonefly hatches that occur on the creek in June and July. Later in the year, I'll switch to something bushy, like an Adams or a fat Royal Trude. In August and September, if you're not fishing a small hopper pattern, you're missing out. All the flies listed here should be in the size 12–16 range, including the hopper.

Gear

In the coming pages, you'll notice similar advice over and over again. Go light. For Moose Creek, I almost always go with a light three-weight rod and a corresponding floating line. If it's windy or if the fish are particularly wary on a given day, I might go with a four-weight—just for a little more casting backbone. But for me, the lighter rod makes for livelier experience when a fish comes to hand.

Moose Creek is a spring creek that bubbles out of the ground at a numbingly cold temperature, and its waters are crystal clear. Normally, I don't fish with light tippet to avoid playing a fish too long and risking injury to it, but Moose Creek's brookies aren't massive (yet they can be leader shy), so I go a little lighter—a 5X tippet seems to be about right.

In high summer, you won't need waders—and honestly, because the creek is pretty small, you likely won't need to get wet at all. I usually fish in shorts and a pair of sandals. The meadow grass around the creek is pretty easy to maneuver, so wading boots aren't vital.

Douse yourself in insect repellant. It's also a good idea to carry bear spray with you—even if you leave it in the car.

Eastern Idaho

Walking across a fallen log over Moose Creek in eastern Idaho.

Location

Moose Creek is located east of Mack's Inn in Island Park. You can find it on page forty-nine of DeLorme's *Idaho Atlas & Gazetteer*.

Bear Creek

I promise that not every stream in Idaho is named for some big, hairy mammal. But Bear Creek clearly is, and it played an important role in the protection of Idaho's backcountry a few years back. It's also a stellar native Yellowstone cutthroat trout fishery.

When Idaho's roadless rule was in draft form, the Bear Creek drainage, a roadless swath of fine fish and game habitat that drains into Palisades Reservoir a stone's flow from the Wyoming line, was proposed for lower-tier protection. Given the creek's importance to native cutthroat trout that run from Palisades Reservoir into the stream to spawn each spring—as well as a corresponding run of brown trout in the fall–Trout Unlimited's Scott Stouder worked with Senator Risch's office and the national roadless area advisory committee to boost the protections for Bear Creek, and he was successful. Now the single-track trail into the Bear Creek backcountry provides access to some of the best small-stream fishing in eastern Idaho, and it'll stay that way for generations to come.

Several years back, I had the chance to walk with Scott into the Bear Creek backcountry for a quick fishing trip. While he'd worked tirelessly to protect this place and others like it, he'd never actually been here. I was anxious to show him what his good work had done for me and countless others who truly value fishing the backcountry.

Armed with a couple fly rods, Scott and I traversed a huge rock moraine at the outset of the trail and wandered up the trail for about

A Yellowstone cutthroat trout from a tributary of Henry's Fork in eastern Idaho.

half an hour. All the while, Scott—who's a passionate big-game hunter—kept his eyes on the ridgelines above us. South-facing slopes with spotted cover reminded him of some of the great mule deer hunts he's experienced in his life, and the Bear Creek drainage, he said, has mule deer written all over it.

We left the single-track trail that's popular with horseback riders and mountain bikers and started a short trek across a field of skunk cabbage toward the creek when Stouder froze. His eyes, glued to the ridgeline well above us and at least a mile away, brightened.

"There's one now," he said, pointing. Sure enough, a large buck traversed a bare patch of sage on the ridge Scott pointed out. It was August, and deer season was months away, but Scott beamed. I think the sight of the deer was actually more rewarding for him than the fishing yet to come, but he didn't say so, perhaps to afraid to offend me, the rabid fly fisher.

"Let's go catch some fish," he said.

Bear Creek is perhaps the stream every backcountry angler envisions when the ideal mountain brook comes to mind. It slices through an alpine valley and runs cold and relatively clear all year long, thanks to ample cover and quality, intact habitat.

As we walked across the meadow of skunk cabbage, grasshoppers took flight and clicked and flitted away from our footsteps. We had adequate imitations tied to our 3X tippet, so when we got to the water, we were ready for the stream's resident cutthroats and, as it turned out, a few larger migratory fish that had lingered into the Bear Creek summer, growing fat on grasshoppers and beefy red ants.

Scott made a single cast and was immediately into a fifteen-inch Yellowstone cutthroat. His four-weight doubled over as the fat fish coursed upstream toward one of the many root-wad snags found along the course of Bear Creek. Scott, a savvy angler, steered the fish back into the current and was able to bring it to hand in short order.

There, with that healthy native fish resting in the palm of his hand, I think both Scott and I took great pride in the work we'd done over the last few years. As the fish slipped back into the current, Scott stood up and took in a deep breath of clean Idaho air. We both knew how special that fish was. And we both knew that, years from now, my children or even my grandchildren could experience this place just as we did that day.

We managed to keep it just like it is for generations to come. It took a lot of work and a lot of help from partners who don't always share the same values, but we got it done. Bear Creek will always be a special place, thanks to the folks who worked to make it so.

Flies

Early in the season, Bear Creek runs a bit off-color due to runoff—it can be a chalky green, and it can really move quickly. But because this is the time of year when the big migratory cutthroats start to show up in the creek, it's very much worth fishing. I'd suggest devolving a bit from the typical backcountry "upstream and dry" mantra. Instead, tie a reasonable replica of a hunk of trout-stream protein on your tippet and swing streamers through deep holes and undercut banks. Typical streamers should work—Woolly Buggers, sculpin imitations, Zonkers and the like will catch the eye of the big migratory fish.

Later in the summer, consider more traditional attractor dry flies, like Adams and Stimulators, or go with a size-fourteen olive Elk-hair Caddis. When August rolls around, there's no excuse to use anything but a terrestrial pattern, preferably a foam ant or hopper imitation that floats high and can hit the water with an appreciative "splat."

When fall comes, go back to streamers. The small run of brown trout from Palisades into Bear Creek won't light your hair on fire, but it's possible to get into some fish in the fifteen- to seventeen-inch range on swung flies.

Gear

For streamers, a stout five-weight with floating line will work just fine, particularly if your fly is weighted a bit. When the dry-fly season comes, scale back—a three- or four-weight rod with corresponding floating line will give you just enough backbone to tackle the odd large cutthroat (say, fifteen to seventeen inches), and it will give the stream's smaller fish a bit more muscle.

You might want waders in the early season and again in the fall, but throughout the summer, wet wading will be much more comfortable. You won't need any fancy footwear—a pair of wading boots or wading sandals that you're OK hiking in will be just fine.

Location

Bear Creek is a tributary of Palisades Reservoir, which impounds the South Fork of the Snake River southeast of Idaho Falls. You can find Bear Creek on page thirty-one of the DeLorme's *Idaho Atlas & Gazetteer*.

Sheridan Creek

The term "private water" instills in many anglers the notion that somehow, because a stream is contained within the boundaries of a stretch of private property, it's simply better. Of course, that's not always true.

Lots of factors play into it, not the least of which is the quality of habitat. In Idaho, much of the bottomland waters are in private hands, and because many of these landowners make their living from the land under their feet, they take very good care of it and manage it for maximum yield, whether that yield be cattle or barley. Others have come to realize the very literal value of a healthy watershed and are working to find ways to keep waters healthy and cold while still running a few cows here and there or raising a hay crop that gives three cuts a year.

Steve Hyde, who manages Sheridan Creek and Eagle Ridge Ranch in Island Park, has helped change the paradigm when it comes to small-stream fishery management for the benefit of recreation, and he's turned Sheridan Creek's Kamloops rainbow trout population into a moneymaker for the ranch's owners.

Now, for clarity, fly fishing private water has always felt a little... dirty. At least to me. In many instances, these waters are contrived impoundments managed solely for the yield of trophy trout that may or may not be replenished by stocked fish or hand-fed pellets to get them through the winter.

I can't speak for how Steve manages Sheridan Creek, but having fished it a couple times in recent years, I can say that it doesn't feel like a private trout tank—it feels like a classic meadow stream that's been

A fat brook trout from eastern Idaho's Sheridan Creek.

saved from the harsh realities of range management and left to recover on its own devices.

I know Steve has worked hard to make improvements to the stream. He's assisted in its recovery from a warm, shallow cattle wallow into what it is today: a truly fantastic small stream chock full of wild fish, albeit nonnative rainbows and some very handsome brook trout.

On a recent September morning, I and a handful of friends heralding from Montana, Idaho and Connecticut all descended on Sheridan Creek for a lazy, late summer day on the water. We strung up light tackle, assuming that we'd be battling ten- to twelve-inch trout in the glistening, clear flow of the little spring creek that bisects Island Park's western third.

Stretches of the stream can indeed be fished on public land (it bubbles from the ground within the boundaries of the Targhee National Forest). But this stretch—this rehabilitated, replenished stretch of Sheridan Creek—has become a true Idaho gem.

And it took the lot of us about five minutes to figure it out. Casting fat foam hopper patterns over the first stretch of likely holding water yielded a quick strike from a nice-sized fish, but I missed the set and managed to snare my fly in a maze of willows behind me. I untangled my mess and, with my three-weight fiberglass rod, made a second cast into the pool. A behemoth rose from the depths and slurped in the hopper pattern without much hesitation. I set the hook, and then all hell broke loose.

I was fishing with Steve Zakur, a great friend of mine and an active member of the Candlewood Valley Chapter of Trout Unlimited in Newtown, Connecticut. Steve had come west for a week of trout fishing in the Yellowstone area, and Steve Hyde was treating us, as well as a few of my TU coworkers, to a day on Sheridan Creek. I remember Steve watching the whole situation unfold—me, woefully underequipped with my favorite little glass rod and a twenty-inch rainbow that just realized the hopper he'd eaten was biting him back.

Steve snapped a couple great photos, including one of me, fish tight to a supple little rod, crashing across the stream to regain a better position and possibly land the fish. It took some time, but I brought the rainbow to hand and felt pretty darn good doing it.

The author battles a big rainbow on light tackle while fishing Sheridan Creek.
Photo by Steve Zakur.

Sated, I watched Zakur and my other buddies chase Sheridan Creek's rainbows and brook trout the rest of the afternoon. Finally, the wind came up and storm clouds appeared on the horizon. We retreated to the bar at Pond's Lodge on the Buffalo River and relived the day in megapixels.

Fly Fishing Idaho's Secret Waters

Greg McReynolds of Pocatello, Idaho, surveys Sheridan Creek in eastern Idaho.

Eastern Idaho

Flies

You'll likely get better advice from the guides and outfitters who work through Eagle Ridge Ranch when it comes to flies, but I think most anglers would gravitate to small-water standbys, like caddis and mayfly imitations in the summer and terrestrials in the late summer and into fall. Streamers will no doubt work as well—the rainbows in Sheridan Creek are very aggressive, and they'll readily chase Woolly Buggers and leech patterns. I'd recommend visiting Sheridan in late summer—it's a great place to be during hopper season.

Gear

Normally, for water this small, I'd recommend light tackle, but there are some legitimate trophies in Sheridan Creek, and to protect the fish—and your tackle—you might consider a five-weight with floating line. You'll get plenty of pull out of Sheridan's trophy trout on the heavier tackle, and you'll be ready when that big Kamloops t-bones your hopper and makes a run downstream.

Location

Sheridan Creek—both the public and the private stretches—can be found on page forty-nine of DeLorme's *Idaho Atlas & Gazetteer*. To fish the private stretch of Sheridan, contact Eagle Ridge Ranch at (208) 558-0900.

Chapter 4
SOUTHERN IDAHO

*I*t's tough to divide Idaho up into regions, given its "pregnant L" shape, but if you had to, southern Idaho would be the largest—and likely the fishiest—portion of the state. From one end of the state to the other, the Snake River carves a lazy horseshoe path across Idaho. From its official formation, where Henry's Fork and the South Fork come together near Menan, to where it leaves Idaho outside of Lewiston and heads downstream through a system of locks and dams on its way to the Columbia, the Snake defines the southern third of the state.

Southern Idaho is also home to storied waters like Silver Creek and the Big Lost River. The Big Wood River, the south and middle forks of the Boise River, the Payette River and the Jarbridge also flow here, and don't forget the Owyhee, which flows wild and free and full of redband rainbows through Idaho. The spring creeks near Hagerman are legendary and full of massive trout, and the small waters that flow from the Owyhees are surprisingly productive and home to some of the purest strains of native redband rainbow trout in the West. Oh, it's plenty fishy, and it's perhaps the best part of the state in which to experience some true diversity. Not only are the tributaries of the Snake and the springs and seeps along the river canyon great trout water, but the river itself has become a trophy smallmouth bass fishery over the last fifteen years or so, and it's one of the best rivers in the West when it comes to fly fishing for carp.

And don't turn up your nose at carp—they're perhaps the most challenging freshwater fish on the fly, and only in recent years have American fly fishers begun to embrace them as worthy fly-rod targets. The Snake and its many backwater bays and shallow flats are carp havens. And aside from chasing steelhead in the Salmon and Clearwater drainages, carp offer Idaho fly anglers the only really good excuse to break the eight-weight out of the closet and make long casts to truly big fish.

And, of course, there are mighty white sturgeon in the Snake—populations have been established all the way upriver beyond Idaho Falls. I don't know anyone who's come up with a dependable way to hook, let alone land, a sturgeon on the fly rod, but I suspect someone's out there giving it a shot.

An angler battles a nice rainbow on southern Idaho's Silver Creek.

The Little Lost River

This hidden little river is one of several "sink" streams in southern Idaho that begin as snowmelt and spring water in the Beaverhead Mountains along the crotch of the "L" in southern Idaho and flow out onto the Big Desert near the much-maligned Idaho National Laboratory. Once these streams (others include Birch Creek and Medicine Bow Creek) hit the porous ground of the desert, they "sink" into the lava-laden earth and don't reappear until they come out of the ground near the Thousand Springs area near Hagerman.

The Little Lost River is one of Idaho's true small-water treasures, and while it's surprisingly accessible, it doesn't see much pressure. For years, my family made a habit of camping at the Mill Creek campground in Sawmill Canyon sometime around the Fourth of July weekend—and we had the campground all to ourselves most of the time.

Home to introduced rainbow and brook trout and the state's most unique population of native bull trout, the Little Lost is perhaps my favorite destination fishery within just a few hours of home in Idaho Falls. The fish in the river's canyon stretch—and the word "river" is misleading—are stunning and can push fifteen inches or so. The rainbows in Sawmill Canyon are absolutely incredible—they sport a deep red stripe down their sides, and they're very aggressive, both when chasing streamers and dry flies.

The brookies, too, are aggressive and very respectable. The river's bull trout are largely relegated to the upper reaches of Sawmill Canyon. Intentionally targeting bull trout in Idaho is illegal, as the fish occupy a spot on the federal Endangered Species List. But in this stretch of water, even when fishing with dry flies (bull trout are notorious piscivores, meaning they eat other fish), catching a bull trout is a very real possibility. And some of these native char get quite large for the water they occupy. A few years back, my son Cameron caught one on a grasshopper pattern that pushed seventeen inches (as per Idaho law, the fish was quickly released).

Southern Idaho

Farther downstream, the river exits Sawmill Canyon and flows south along a stretch of idyllic Western landscape dotted with sage. In this stretch, the fish get a bit bigger, and trophy trout fishing becomes a real possibility, particularly for rainbows.

But for me, it's the backcountry stretch of the Little Lost and a couple of its tributaries that draw me back year after year. High in the river's headwaters, the road up Sawmill Canyon comes to an end, and the only way to get to the water is to walk among the willows and the downed timber left behind from a fire some years back. The river—little more than a trickle by late summer—is alive with feisty rainbow trout and bull trout, both of which will hit high-floating dry flies with little hesitation.

Cameron Hunt shows off a native bull trout he caught using a tenkara rod on the Little Lost River.

This is where my son, Cameron, learned how to use a tenkara fly rod—a Japanese fly rod that's long and supple and doesn't have a reel. In my opinion, it's a great fly fishing teaching tool and a very effective method of fishing small water.

Cameron's tenkara rod is eleven feet long, and the specialized line connected to a "lillian" at the rod tip is about twelve feet long. This form of fly fishing allows the angler, in close quarters, to present a fly to wary fish with nothing but the fly on the water. And without a reel or the need to manage line, it removes some of the complexities from the craft without taking away from the enjoyment of fly fishing.

Cameron was ten years old when he and I made the drive to the Little Lost. As we wandered among the willows, we spooked a cow moose and her calf—thankfully at a safe distance—and watched for a time as one of the stream's many beavers repaired a leaky dam, courtesy of a late-summer deluge the day before.

In time, my son was handling the Japanese rod without any assistance from me, and when he connected with his first bull-trout—a beautiful ten-inch fish that hit a Royal Coachman in a foot of water—he beamed from under the brim of his hat.

We fished the upper reaches of the river most of afternoon and into the evening, wandering well away from the end of the road and relishing a slice of Idaho backcountry that will remain special to both of us for years to come.

There are some unique aspects of fishing the sinks that most anglers won't consider—not because they're not interested but because the natural history of these waters is not well known.

First, it's likely that at least some of the sink's drainages were fishless before trout were introduced into them. Second, there's an ongoing debate over how bull trout ended up in the Little Lost River. Technically, there's no connection between the Little Lost and the Snake River below Shoshone Falls (where bull trout would be considered native). The explanations vary.

The notion I prefer to believe is that, at one time, eons ago, the Little Lost River was actually a tributary to the Pahsimeroi River, which flows north into the Salmon River, where bull trout are native. It's possible that some geological event (this portion of Idaho is seismically lively, and some of the nearby lava fields are only two thousand years old) separated the Little Lost (and its fish) from the Pahsimeroi, creating an isolated population of bull trout in the Little Lost River.

Rachel Morgan fishes the headwaters of the Little Lost River in southern Idaho.

The other explanation is much less romantic (but just as likely, if not more so). Years ago, when the first settlers came to the Little Lost River Valley, it's possible that they transplanted fish from the Pahsimeroi into the fishless Little Lost. That would explain the presence of bull trout and, perhaps, the rainbows. (Are the Little Lost's rainbows the progeny of Salmon River steelhead?) The river's brook trout are likely the product of an organized introduction effort on the part of fisheries managers years and years ago.

Either way, bull trout live in this isolated drainage, and they enjoy the protection they deserve in these waters. For me—and for my son—this place is magical. If you ever have the chance, I'll wager you'll find the Little Lost to be just as special.

A redband rainbow trout pulled from the Wind River.

Flies

The Little Lost's trout aren't terribly picky—a theme you'll find among most backcountry trout. Early in the season, try swinging a wet fly like a Rio Grande King or a Stayner Ducktail through runoff-swollen water. As the summer progresses, switch to attractor dries, like Stimulators, Adams and Royal Coachmans. Later in the summer, particularly in the valley of the river, go with high-floating foam hoppers, beetles and ants. Higher up, simply use smaller versions—the terrestrial hatch all along the Little Lost in late summer is prolific.

Gear

For streamers and fat hoppers, use a five-weight with floating line. Higher up, go light with a three- or four-weight rod and floating line. If you're interested in giving it a try, use a tenkara rod. The Little Lost is the ideal experimental laboratory for this method of fly fishing, and if you're like me, once you try it, you'll want to keep trying it.

Location

The Little Lost River is a sinks stream that flows south out of the Beaverhead Mountains toward the little village of Howe, Idaho. It can be found on pages thirty-eight, thirty-nine and forty-six of DeLorme's *Idaho Atlas & Gazetteer*.

The Carp Flats of the Snake River

Certainly, no one in their right mind would claim the Snake as a "secret water," but I do believe that most Idaho anglers forsake the Snake when it comes to what I believe to be the most game freshwater fish in America—even if carp are considered trash fish by most American anglers. I also hold to the notion that carp are perhaps the ideal freshwater fish for fly-rodders; as their general wariness combined with their liberal diet provides challenge and opportunity all at once.

Carp, first introduced into American waters under the Ulysses S. Grant administration, were brought in as a source of protein for a developing nation. Since they were first stocked in a pond in Maryland in the 1860s, they've spread to every state in the Lower 48. Idaho enjoys a thriving population, particularly in the carp-friendly waters of the Snake River as it flows along the state's southern third.

I first stumbled upon carp in the Snake in the early 2000s. I'd crossed the dam at American Falls and wandered down a lonely gravel road more often used by farmers and ranchers along the river's northern banks than by anglers or even hunters who might find deer, moose and pronghorn in this vast desert landscape. I was actually following the directions to a promising place on the river to chase smallmouth bass—a fish that, at the time, was gaining quite a following in southern Idaho and one that has since become a treasured fly-rod target in its own right on the Snake.

And while I didn't find any smallies that day, I was shocked at the numbers of big carp wallowing in two feet of water. They jumped and tailed and generally worked up a frenzy as they prepared to spawn that glorious May afternoon.

Carp start showing up on the shallow-water flats of the Snake in late March, particularly in the river's downstream reaches near Mountain Home and C.J. Strike Reservoir. By mid-April, a bright, sunny day with temperatures in the seventies will bring them up to the flats farther upstream near Raft River and on up to American Falls on the edges of Eastern Idaho.

Cameron Hunt admires a big carp pulled from southern Idaho's Snake River.

These Asia natives will start to spawn in earnest around the first of June and continue for a few weeks, concluding in July. They'll remain on the flats—or move back and forth from deeper water to feed—throughout the summer.

The attraction of carp on the river's flats—at least to me—is that they behave a lot like treasured saltwater fish. They tail and root around for crustaceans, just like redfish. They cruise in hungry pods, just like bonefish. And they can be incredibly selective, like permit. Like all of the above, carp are strong, fast fish prone to reel-whistling runs and shattered graphite.

And, of course, I don't have to spend a small fortune or two days' worth of travel time to get to the places they swim.

No, the backwater flats of Snake River aren't the crystalline flats of the Bahamas, but they possess their own beauty, one that's grown on me over time. The lava bluffs overlooking the green waters of the Snake take my breath away every time I lay eyes on them. And to drive along the river and see these massive invaders—sometimes pushing thirty pounds—breaching the frothy surface is a treat only an angler willing to expand his fishy horizons can appreciate.

I remember that as a kid living in suburban Denver, carp were really the only fish I could dependably catch within range of my banana-seat bicycle or the soles of my sneakers. Using bread dough concocted in my mother's kitchen and sunk to the bottom of the lake at Stern Park, carp prodded my imagination and scratched that fishy itch until I could find a ride with my grandfather into the Colorado high country to chase brookies, browns and rainbows in the cold, clean water of the Rockies.

Today, convincing them to hit a fly is much more challenging than snoozing on the bank and waiting for one to suck in a dough ball past the barbels. And—perish the thought!—I honestly believe that for sheer pleasure, I'd rather latch into a carp on the flats than I would the average trout.

Blasphemy? For a trout purist, certainly. But for a wandering fly fisher with an itch to experiment, no. That's not to say there's no guilt involved. It's hardly an altruistic endeavor, chasing carp on the fly.

Matt Woodard of Idaho Falls pulls a big carp out of the Snake River.

But it also doesn't help that carp are nonnative and generally make a mess of things. Unfortunately, short of a nuclear explosion (and even then, I wonder) in southern Idaho, they're here to stay. They make up a frightening percentage of the biomass in the Snake and in waters all across America, from the Great Lakes to southern Florida.

I choose to adapt, much as carp have done, to some of the new, alien environments here in Idaho, knowing, of course, that there remain some untouched little gems where things are just as they should be.

Flies

On the Snake, carp enjoy an omnivorous existence. Early in the year, just as they arrive on the flats and start to push into the reeds in search of food, they're mostly after damselfly and dragonfly nymphs. These bugs swim, and carp chase them. To mimic these large nymphs, I've used (with great success) a Stayner Ducktail. The olive body and mottled ducktail give just the right feel to the fly when stripped slowly through shallow water. Later, as the water warms, any reasonable imitation of a crawfish will likely work. When sight-fishing for cruising carp with crawfish patterns, cast well ahead of the expected route of the fish and let the fly sink. Only when the fish is a foot or so away from the fly should you give it a twitch.

Streamers, such as Woolly Buggers, leech patterns and sculpin imitations, can work as well. Carp are the most vulnerable, and thus most forgiving, when they're tailing. Putting flies right on them will work when they're obviously in a feeding mood.

Gear

Early in the year, you might like a pair of waders, but as spring turns into summer, you'll be happier wading wet, even on the sometimes-creepy mudflats of the Snake. To better your chances and cover more water, consider a one-person pontoon craft that you can control with flippers on your feet. You'll stir up less water and have more freedom to look for fish.

As for rods, I'd recommend fishing a seven-weight at minimum. The wind across the Snake River Plain is unforgiving, and for that reason, I almost always fish a stout, saltwater-worthy eight-weight with floating line. There are times, when the fish aren't quite up in the shallows, that a sink-tip or an intermediate sink-tip line would be appropriate, but most carp anglers I know fish with floating line exclusively.

> ### *Location*
>
> This one's pretty much up to you. I've caught carp at a number of public access points along the river, ranging from American Falls all the way downstream to Mountain Home. One way to find flats on the river is to cruise its length in the winter, when the Department of Reclamation is holding water back in the river's reservoirs. This lowers the river's level, and you'll be able to identify flats because they'll likely be exposed. Roads and access points along the Snake can be found on pages nineteen, twenty, twenty-one, twenty-four, twenty-five, twenty-six and twenty-nine in DeLorme's *Idaho Atlas & Gazetteer*.

JORDAN CREEK

If you live in Idaho, you've heard the tale of Claude Dallas, the antifederalist who shot and killed two Idaho Fish and Game wardens in remote Owyhee County in 1981. He remained at large for over a year, finally coming to justice in April 1982 outside of Winnemucca, Nevada. He was charged and convicted of voluntary manslaughter and sent to prison. In 1986, Dallas escaped and went on the lam again. He was found in suburban Southern California about a year later and returned to Idaho to serve out his time. He was released from prison in 2005.

I've always wondered about the fascination many Idahoans have with Dallas, who among many is considered a modern-day folk hero. Truth be told, he is exactly what he went to prison for: a criminal who took the lives of two men who were simply doing their jobs. Dallas fashioned a life

REWARD
UP TO
$20,000

For information leading to the Arrest and Conviction of
CLAUDE LAFAYETTE DALLAS, JR.
for the Murder of two Idaho Fish and Game Officers on January 5, 1981.

- Date of Birth: 3-11-50
- Height: 5' 10"
- Weight: 180 lbs.
- Brown Hair (may be shoulder length)
- Brown Eyes
- May have full beard
- Wears glasses
- Social Security No. 270-49-0296

Subject is an accomplished trapper and shooter.

SUBJECT IS ARMED AND EXTREMELY DANGEROUS.

CONTACT —
Sheriff Tim Nettleton, Owyhee County, Idaho - Murphy, Idaho 83650 — (208) 495-2441

DALLAS, CLAUDE LAFAYETTE, JR.

Date of Birth: 3-11-50
Place of Birth: Winchester, Virginia
5' 10", 180 lbs.
Brown Hair (long, wears ponytail), Brown Eyes.
Full Beard, Wears Glasses.
N.C.I.C. Entry No. W247288563
S.S. No. 270-49-0296
F.B.I. No. 208406 MI
N.C.I.C. F.P.C. 12AA0807041652061308
No known scars or marks.

off the land in the remote reaches of the Owyhees, and he was, bluntly put, a poacher who trapped and hunted illegally, seasons be damned.

Perhaps the romance that often accompanies the Dallas story has to do with his disdain for authority or his general lack of respect for societal norms or the system of rules and regulations put in place to protect Idaho's fish and game for the rest of us who live here. I don't buy into Dallas as a folk hero. He shirked his duty as an American and dodged the Vietnam draft. Then he disappeared into the wild and withdrew from Idaho's fish and game bounty without once making a constructive deposit.

I'll never understand how a jury refused to convict Dallas of murder—the two officers who tried to arrest him for poaching were each shot twice, once with a pistol he had strapped to his leg and again with a rifle, execution style. I find it even more sickening that Dallas's tale was immortalized by folksinger Tom Russell. If all it takes to achieve immortality these days is to live off the land, I know plenty of men I'd consider more heroic than some recluse who'd take the lives of two game wardens in cold blood. There are respectable people today who live off game and fish harvested legally, within the rules we put in place to protect Idaho's priceless fish and wildlife. And they haven't executed a single game warden.

Dallas was released from prison in 2005, and today, his whereabouts are largely unknown. It is known that he obtained a driver's license in Washington State in 2005, and according to Dan Popkey, a columnist with the *Idaho Statesman*, rumors of late include that he's working summers as a shuttle driver for rafting trips along the Payette River. In the fall of 2007, also according to the *Idaho Statesman*, there were reports that he was seen in Jordan Valley, Oregon.

The whole Dallas drama occurred well to the south and west of the historic mining town of Silver City, but it was in this eclectic little town that I was reminded of this episode. My fishing buddy Rachel Morgan and I were exploring the region last summer when, at the Idaho Hotel and Bar, I saw one of the old "wanted" posters for Dallas hanging on the wall.

A circa 1981 "wanted" poster for Claude Dallas.

A wily Jordan Creek redband rainbow trout comes to hand on the cups of Idaho's remote Owyhees.

Slicing through Silver City is a quiet little stream. Jordan Creek starts above town and flows right by old tailings piles and abandoned old cars that add charm to this remote southern Idaho tourist destination. And in Jordan Creek resides a population of redband rainbow trout that get almost no attention from the locals (or visitors, for that matter).

It's understandable. They're diminutive little fish, and they spook at the most subtle movement. From the gravel road paralleling the creek leading into town, you can see pods of these fish, the largest maybe ten inches long, finning in the sheltered, clear waters of Jordan Creek.

And they can be caught, but it isn't easy.

Rachel and I spent a day walking quietly among the aspens, cottonwoods and willows of Jordan Creek. I fished a tenkara rod in hopes of keeping fly line off the water—and in tight quarters, I wanted a limited backcast. In what amounted to several hours chasing these little redbands, I managed to bring two to hand. And I felt damned good about it. Rachel, fishing with conventional fly tackle, had similar success—or failure, depending on how you look at it.

I've asked myself a dozen times since that day on Jordan Creek why I felt compelled to run around the creek bottoms and chase tiny native trout. After much reflection, I suppose I'd have to consider where these precious little gems live.

I first laid eyes on them as a pod of these fish rose to a midge hatch beneath a building that actually spans the creek. At the time, I figured them easy pickings, as rising trout in small water are not known to be the wariest of fish.

But hours later, scratched from bushwhacking through tight stands of willows and burning from a run-in with stinging nettle along the creek, I was beyond delighted to cradle a six-inch redband in my hand. The effort was stupendous, and while the reward was tiny, it was hardly unappreciated.

There are rumors of little creeks and ponds all through the Owyhees—as well as the fabled Owyhee River itself—that hold populations of willing redbands. One day, I'll journey farther into the wild, to the lands where Claude Dallas etched out a criminal existence.

Perhaps I'll grow to appreciate the convict—but I doubt it.

Flies

It's not so much a matter of flies on Jordan Creek as it is a matter of presentation. As I said, these little fish are really wary, and they retreat under rocks and into the dark depths of the creek at the slightest movement. When I was able to put a fly in front of fish I hadn't yet spooked, it didn't seem to matter what flavor of dry it was. But if I failed to connect with a strike, which was the norm and not the exception, I didn't get a second chance.

That being said, I'd stick with tried-and-true dries, like a small size-eighteen Adams or a similar attractor. A caddis imitation, tied small, will likely work on these tiny trout, and in later summer, small terrestrials will work, too.

Gear

I think the tenkara rod (I fished a supple, eleven-foot Japanese fly rod) was the right tool for the job. It allowed me to put a fly on the water while keeping the line elevated. Waders aren't necessary, as the creek is quite shallow. But long pants should be worn because of the brush, branches and the presence of stinging nettle.

Location

Jordan Creek flows through the little town of Silver City. It can be found on page twenty-four of DeLorme's *Idaho Atlas & Gazetteer*.

Chapter 5
CENTRAL IDAHO

This is the home of the fabled River of No Return—the mighty Salmon. It runs from the top of Idaho—elevation-wise—at the top of Galena Summit and meanders some two hundred miles, disappearing into the wilderness below the town of North Fork and reappearing about twenty miles above the town of Riggins.

Today, it's home to some of the last salmon and steelhead runs in Idaho—the fish that return from the ocean and make it to the Sawtooth Fish Hatchery above Stanley have come better part of one thousand miles to spawn and die.

As you might suspect, though, there's more to the waters of central Idaho than the Salmon River itself. It's a fishy paradise for both anadromous fish and wild trout and char among tall ponderosas and steep, tall country that steals your breath and instills in anglers everywhere the wonder that inspires them to poke into unknown canyons or follow unnamed trickles, fly rod in hand.

The Middle Fork of the Salmon is perhaps the most storied wilderness float trip in the Lower 48 today. Boaters who make the trip are in for about a week of off-the-grid floating and fishing for native westslope

cutthroat trout. And the fishing is, as a friend of mine who did the float just a couple years ago said, "ridiculous."

A trip down the Middle Fork must be done either through a licensed outfitter or an applied permit process. The permits are few and far between—only seven permits are granted each day between the end of May and the beginning of September, and they're awarded on a lottery-based drawing. For many people, it's a once-in-a-lifetime experience.

The Salmon is the lifeblood of central Idaho and part of what my friend Scott Stouder—who lives just outside of the river town of Riggins—calls the "heartbeat of the Columbia River salmon run." Coupled with the Clearwater River system of northern Idaho, the state has some stellar spawning and rearing habitat for salmon and steelhead. The challenge lies in the dams along the Lower Snake River and the Columbia. For smolts that travel hundreds of miles to the ocean—tail first—these slack waters make for a perilous journey. The return trip isn't much easier, given that there are five dams on the Lower Snake River alone that they must traverse.

The author looks for steelhead in the headwaters of the Salmon River in the shadows of the Sawtooths. *Photo by Brett Prettyman.*

Sadly, the dams serve little sensible value. They afford the city of Lewiston "port city" status, as barges can come and go, but it could be argued that the dams cost too much to maintain to make the port of Lewiston economically worthwhile. Additionally, the dams contribute a miniscule amount of power to the Northwest grid, making that argument somewhat moot as well.

It's likely that salmon and steelhead will never return to the Salmon River in the numbers they once did until the dams on the Lower Snake come out. Politically and culturally, that's a heavy lift. Ecologically, and some would say economically, it's a no-brainer.

But fishing in this part of Idaho is still amazing, and as I said, not just on the Salmon itself. Other less-heralded waters thrive in the shadow of the River of No Return, and for anglers who like to get off the pavement, this part of Idaho is a great place to get lost for a day—or a week. This might be the best of Idaho.

The Salmon is a huge drainage, and it collects hundreds of tributary streams from its source above Stanley to its confluence with the Snake along the Oregon border. At its source in the shadow of the Sawtooths, it flows through some of the most severe alpine habitat in the country. Once it charges off of the alpine bowl that contains the town of Stanley—and after collecting dozens of little mountain trickles—the Salmon becomes a furious river that just keeps collecting water.

Among the first sizable streams it collects is the Lemhi River. This river starts atop

A westslope cutthroat trout from the Pack River in northern Idaho.

Lemhi Pass, which is significant because it's the site where Meriwether Lewis first crossed the Continental Divide on August 12, 1805, making him the first U.S. citizen to cross the spine of America. There, standing atop Lemhi Pass, he could see still more high mountains in the distance, some still covered with snow even in mid-August.

It must have been daunting to think that he and his expedition had arrived at the headwaters of the Columbia River only to see how much severe terrain lay between them and their goal of reaching the ocean. But the significance wasn't lost on Lewis. He topped the pass and wrote the following about his next move: "I now descended the mountain about ¾ of a mile, which I found steeper than on the opposite side, to a handsome bold running Creek of cold clear water. Here I first tasted the water of the great Columbia river."

Not only was Lewis the first European-American to cross the divide, he was also the first to drink from the waters of the mighty Salmon River drainage.

While Lewis was the first in the expedition to visit Idaho, the party didn't travel down the Salmon to the Snake and then to Columbia. After visiting with the Lemhi Shoshones, Lewis went back into Montana over the aptly named Lost Trail Pass, which follows the North Fork of the Salmon River back up to the headwaters of two great Montana waters: the Bitterroot and the Big Hole.

From there, the expedition eventually crossed back into Idaho over Lolo Pass in northern Idaho. Its members then followed the Lochsa River down to the Clearwater and eventually into the Snake and on to the Pacific.

Today, not too far from where the North Fork enters the main Salmon, the road along the river ends, and the river enters the wilderness. It truly is the River of No Return.

Hazard Creek

The first time I fished Hazard Creek, my family and I had ventured over to the home of Scott Stouder and Holly Endersby—two great friends who devote their lives to protecting wild Idaho. Scott and Holly own a home atop the ridge that separates the Rapid River from the Little Salmon River near the river town of Riggins, and they run a pack string of horses and mules they use each summer and fall for backcountry hunting and fishing trips.

We arrived at their house just in time to help them bring in the last of their hay that July, and after toiling in the field for a few hours, we drove down off the mountain and wandered up Hazard Creek, a tributary to the Little Salmon.

It's not a particularly hidden stream—there's actually a sign for Hazard Creek right off of Highway 95. The Little Salmon is a quality salmon and steelhead stream, and it doesn't get a lot of attention for its resident population of redbands and westslope cutthroat trout. The same holds true for Hazard Creek. Within ten minutes of leaving the pavement on a good gravel road, my wife, daughter and I were gloriously alone, parked in a makeshift campsite that's likely used more by elk than it is anglers.

Earlier that year, my wife had given me my first tenkara rod—at my request, of course. I'd been hearing a lot about the supple Japanese fly-fishing method and was anxious to give it a try. It wasn't too long before I'd stumbled across a video for tenkara fishing. Not long after that, I watched a friend from Leadville, Colorado, put a tenkara rod to use catching greenback cutthroats in a tiny stream in the Holy Cross Wilderness. I knew that, for the type of fishing I loved to do, the tenkara rod would be the next step in my evolution as an angler.

But the tenkara baffled me. It was eleven feet long. It had no reel. It's "fly line" was braided nylon, and the line itself was ten feet long. In my hands, it felt foreign. Its simplicity was too…complicated.

Naturally, my wife awarded me with a tenkara rod for my birthday, and it sat in its diminutive case for a couple months until the weather warmed enough to justify a backcountry trip. I cautiously packed the little telescoping rod in its tiny little tube and placed it carefully in my backpack. In the other rod holder, I packed my favorite backcountry fiberglass beauty—a soft, slow three-weight creek rod that casts like a champ but gives even small backcountry trout their due.

I arrived at the trailhead and wandered into the backcountry until I felt I was far enough away from civilization that I wouldn't encounter another angler. I propped my pack on a streamside rock and began to take in the water. I identified likely holding runs in the swift-moving canyon stream—pockets of fishy water where trout no doubt waited in ambush for the current to deliver the next meal. These were long slicks of soft water where, had the light been a little better, I'm sure I would have been able to see finning backcountry rainbows lying patiently in wait for the next unsuspecting mayfly.

I reached for the tenkara, but at the last second, I chickened out and strung up the three-weight. Confidence. In the little creek rod, I oozed confidence. In the long, supple Japanese import, I had none.

The tale relived itself over and over for the next month or so. I'd bring the tenkara with me, but I'd fish with conventional fly gear.

But it was here on Hazard Creek that I became inspired. My wife can generally be credited with my fly-fishing vice—she gave me my first truly good fly rod twenty years ago, and I've slipped slowly into a fishy coma since. And as the three of us stood around the hatchback of the family SUV eyeing fly rods (it was just me and the girls because Cameron was spending a week at summer camp in McCall), I instinctively pulled out my little three-weight.

"Are you going to use the tenkara rod?" my wife asked. I shook my head.

"Do you mind if I try it?"

I removed the rod from its case and unveiled the delicate instrument. I noticed my wife looking at the rod intently. I stretched the telescoping sections to its full eleven-foot length and handed it to her. My daughter, also along on this little adventure, was quick to speak up. "Can I try

Rico Roberts of Nampa, Idaho, fishes Hazard Creek in central Idaho.

it, Mommy?" she asked. Wife and daughter disappeared into the alders to ply the little creek with the long rod. I strung up the three-weight and wandered to the stream, relieved but a little disappointed that I had once again remained firmly boxed into my comfort zone.

I fished for a few minutes, and I generally had my way with the creek's pan-sized redbands—and I hooked (but didn't land) a bull trout that might have stretched the tape to sixteen inches or so. Finally, my curiosity got the best of me. I walked upstream to where I had last seen the girls.

Over the din of a rushing Hazard Creek, I could hear the sound of sheer joy. Giggles. Shouts. Pure laughter. I stepped through the alders on the creek's bank and spied my wife standing on a rock midstream, the long tenkara rod stretched out from her hands. She'd cast the rod slightly upstream and let the high-floating Adams drift along a current seam not ten feet from where she stood. On nearly every cast of the long, supple rod, a small redband would charge the fly, triggering a shout of glee.

Unfamiliar with the rod's slow action, she wouldn't hook a fish on every cast, but she'd make contact. And the opportunistic fish that almost never see a fly weren't shy at all. If she missed a fish mid-drift, she'd simply leave the fly on the water and let it go all the way below her, where she'd then skate it over a slick just before the creek tumbled over a rock on its way to the next small rapid. There, she would almost certainly hook up.

Then it dawned on me. Tenkara fishing is not a fly-fishing evolution; it's the opposite—a return to something much more basic. Sure, it's constructed of high-modulus graphite and conveniently telescopes into a tube about the size of Harry Potter's wand. But it's a devolution—an escape from terminology that, to the inexperienced fly fisher, seems meant to confound and complicate. Line weights, rod lengths, action, flex—no wonder our sport can intimidate newcomers and has a tweedy, snooty reputation.

But the tenkara is different. It's perhaps the most basic form of angling, right up there with dunking a worm off a bridge over some sleepy, slow southern river in hopes of latching into a big catfish. The only difference is that it brings with it the fly-fishing spirit. It's a moving-water endeavor, where rock-hopping and pioneering pay dividends. It's a simple combination of the fly-fishing soul and the effortlessness that comes with dropping a worm to the bottom of the river.

And watching my wife and, later, my daughter enjoy something that has gripped my spirit for two decades brought a deeply satisfying feeling to my heart. Hearing the laughter and seeing the smiles stretching across their faces was one of the best moments of my fishing life.

And yes, the next time I meandered into the backcountry, I left the three-weight in the truck and got to know the simple joy of tenkara angling.

I may never give up my arsenal of fly rods, but I have stepped out into a new realm of fly fishing. It's one where I worry less about perfection. Less about mechanics. Less about the fishing. Instead, it's more about the water and the finned critters that are my target. I've come to truly love the tenkara craft and the basic bliss that comes with connecting to a wild trout in a wild place.

And it all happened on Hazard Creek.

Flies

The redbands and the occasional westslope cutthroat in Hazard Creek are happy to chase attractor dry flies all summer long, but larger specimens will hit streamers, like Zonkers and Muddler Minnows. The creek does have a resident population of bull trout, and larger bull trout will migrate into Hazard Creek in August in preparation for the fall spawn, and these fish will hit a streamer, too. Remember, it's illegal to target bull trout in Idaho, and if you catch one, be sure to release it unharmed.

Gear

As noted above, Hazard Creek is a great stream to fish tenkara. But if that's not your style, I'd recommend a four-weight with enough backbone to strip small streamers through the deeper holes while still being light enough so that you can enjoy the uber-willing redbands on dry flies. You might like a pair of waders early in the year, but Hazard Creek carries a lot of snowmelt out of the Grass Mountains to the east, and it's often not fishable until July. By then, the weather in the canyon has warmed up appreciably, and you'll be refreshed by the creek's cool water on your bare shins.

Location

Hazard Creek runs into the Little Salmon River north of Riggins. It can be found in DeLorme's *Idaho Atlas & Gazetteer* on pages fifty and fifty-one.

Bear Valley

Living in Idaho Falls and sending your kids to summer camp on the shores of Payette Lake just north of McCall is a bit…unwieldy. No matter how you slice it, it's an eight-hour drive from one side of Idaho to the other—straight highways are nonexistent in this state, and there are lots of "you can't get there from here" moments, to be sure.

So, as my son Cameron and I set off for McCall a few summers back to go and retrieve his sister from the grips of the Episcopal church camp amid the ponderosas and the cedars of central Idaho, we decided we'd drive as far as we could across Idaho on gravel roads.

We ventured up the Big Lost River to Mackay and then cut west on gravel roads, following the river into the fabled Copper Basin. We then topped Trail Creek Pass and dropped down into Sun Valley and the headwaters of the Big Wood, where we checked out the Hemingway Memorial and enjoyed a late lunch. We then topped Galena Summit and entered the headwaters of the Salmon River drainage.

We lingered at the Sawtooth Fish Hatchery—it was July, and a good run of chinook salmon were arriving at the hatchery after swimming nearly nine hundred miles from the salt. Cameron might have been seven at the time, and I'll never forget his reaction to every fish that breached the surface of the river that day—it was like watching a fireworks show.

It truly is a remarkable sight, no matter how you feel about hatcheries and dams and the generally sad state of Idaho's salmon and steelhead runs. Watching a massive fish that was born in this water come back after a journey of nine hundred miles to the Pacific and then likely thousands of more miles up the coast of British Columbia and southeast Alaska—perhaps as far as the tip of the Aleutians or even as far as Russia—come back to this little sweet spot in the heart of Idaho is indeed incredible.

And watching a child soak in the enormity of that moment was no less special.

A Bear Valley Creek rainbow trout.

Rather than push on, we stayed overnight in Stanley, which sits in bowl beneath the stunning Sawtooths to the west and the Boulder and White Cloud mountains to the east. This is the "top of Idaho," in terms of general elevation. Borah Peak is to the south and is the state's highest mountain, at 12,662 feet, but this basin, where the Salmon River collects water from five recognized ranges—the Sawtooths, the White Clouds, the Boulders, the Smoky Mountains and the Boise Mountains—would be near the very top if Idaho were a pyramid. Stanley itself sits at 6,300 feet, and the locals are fond of both of its seasons—winter and the Fourth of July.

Cameron and I enjoyed a burger for dinner that evening while overlooking the Salmon. His first glimpse of the returning chinooks inspired him, and he had his eyes glued to the river. Every so often, just to impress his dad, I think, his eyes would brighten and he'd point at the water with a mouthful of fries and shout, "There's one!"

We got up early the next morning and drove north and west out of Stanley, with the Sawtooths towering over us. Living in the shadow of the

Tetons in eastern Idaho, I'm no stranger to dramatic vistas, but there's something about the Sawtooths that sends chills down my spine. For a few years in a row, a group of us visited Stanley every spring to sight-cast to massive steelhead as they completed their journey home from the ocean. And while it was magical to coax one of these amazing fish to the fly, the sight of the Sawtooths outside the cabin every morning was enough to satiate even the most cynical angler.

We once again left the pavement, turning onto Bear Valley Road—we wouldn't see the blacktop again until we got to the little village of Knox on the shores of Warm Lake. From there, it was an easy drive west to Cascade and then another quick drive to McCall.

But that little stretch of gravel crosses some of the best of Idaho. It slices right through Bear Valley, which is crisscrossed with little streams like Fir Creek, Elk Creek, Wyoming Creek and Bear Valley Creek. We stopped often, hitting a number of the small waters with light fly tackle. For Cameron, it was his first real fly-fishing adventure, and it was the first time he willingly left my side and explored. He caught little rainbows and brook trout on high-floating dries, and he wandered through the willows, hopping from one bend in the creek to another.

Bear Valley Creek is the largest of the streams in the valley, and Cameron and I spent the better part of the afternoon chasing pan-sized rainbow and brookies in this meandering stream.

We rounded a bend on the stream and came upon a wild salmon redd, swept clean by a female chinook and occupied by two massive salmon. We stopped fishing and watched intently as the next generation of wild salmon was conceived in these cold waters, so far away from the ocean. For me, the experience was much more profound than watching the big fish come back to the hatchery. Here, after topping all five Lower Snake River dams and charging up Dagger Falls, these huge, nearly spent fish performed one last dutiful act. It was bittersweet, of course. Fifty years ago, this gorgeous little alpine stream might have hosted a hundred salmon redds and thousands of big chinooks. On this day, we saw two.

Delaney Hunt fishes Fir Creek in Bear Valley.

I'll never forget those two lonely fish. I hope that one day, we'll come to our senses and remove the obstacles that keep Idaho from enjoying its fishy legacy. Perhaps a generation from now, Cameron can bring my grandchildren to Bear Valley Creek, and they can count salmon in the hundreds.

A guy can dream.

Flies

The trout in Bear Valley's diminutive waters aren't very selective, and I'd recommend the usual collection of attractor dry patterns and Elk-hair caddis patterns. Later in the summer, terrestrial ant and beetle patterns will bring the larger rainbows and brook trout to the top. Keep your eyes peeled for the big chinooks starting sometime in July, and do your best to avoid them as they produce the next generation of Idaho's salmon.

Gear

The waters of Bear Valley are ideal for light fly tackle, and for the most part, they're meadow streams, making for easy casting and generally easy fishing. You might like some waders early in the season, but I prefer to wade these streams wet—if I wade at all. Most of the good holding water can be reached from the bank, and that reduces the chances of accidentally stumbling upon spawning salmon or spoiling a salmon redd.

Location

Bear Valley is located northwest of Stanley and can be found on pages forty-three and forty-four of DeLorme's *Idaho Atlas & Gazetteer*.

The Wind River

Not to be confused with the mighty Wind River of Wyoming, this little tributary to the main Salmon River about twenty miles east of Riggins is a snakey, low-elevation stream that's bursting at the seams with native redbands, a few westslope cutthroats and the occasional bull trout.

I first fished the Wind with Scott Stouder and both of my kids—a testament to the ease of fishing, once you get through the brush to the creek itself. It's an "end of the road" fishery, and to get to it requires a bit of effort, including a walk across a footbridge spanning the Salmon and a short hike into the Gospel Hump Wilderness.

On our first visit to the Wind, Cameron—maybe six years old at the time—came upon a chukar on the trail into the wilderness, and he decided he'd try and catch the bird. He gave chase and got surprisingly close before the prized game bird took flight and disappeared into the ponderosas down by the edge of the Salmon River.

Delaney, then all of ten years old, laughed at her brother and sprinted ahead of him on the trail, hoping to come across another of the Asian imports that thrive among the severe terrain of the lower Salmon River country.

Within minutes of reaching the shore, both kids were in the cold, clear water—it gets hot along the Salmon in the summertime, and tributaries like the Wind offer folks a chance to cool off.

Minutes later, casting Yellow Humpies in the fast current, both kids had landed pan-sized redbands and were on the way to maybe the best fishing day of their lives. It was also the first time either of my kids had actually harvested trout for the grill. The limit for trout is two fish in the region, so we were able to be pretty picky and take

A Wind River bull trout.

home only the largest of the dozens of redband rainbows we each caught that day.

The Wind is a high-gradient stream—it falls over boulders and spills into plunge pools all along its length. The native redbands and a smattering of native westslope cutthroats inhabit these little pools, and in the bigger, deeper runs, native bull trout—both resident and those that migrate in from the Salmon—can be found, particularly later in the summer as they prepare for the fall spawn.

Toward the stream's confluence with the Salmon River, it rushes across a boulder field, and this is where larger redbands and bull trout will hit streamers. As you hit the actual wedding of the Wind and Salmon Rivers, it's even possible to latch into a smallmouth bass—these nonnative predators are at home in the Salmon's warm summer waters.

Later that evening, sitting on the deck at Scott and Holly's ridge-top home overlooking the Rapid River canyon, Scott fired up the grill. Minutes later, both kids tasted the fruits of their fishing that day. The trout cooked up well and was perfectly supplemented by a garden salad and a baked potato.

I've since returned to Wind River, and I've yet to be disappointed by the fishing. Some years, the cutthroats seem to be a bit more prevalent than others, but the redbands are always there and always dependable. On the stream's lower reaches, it's possible to hook a small redband and then watch as, from the depths, a two-foot-long bull trout appears, trying to make a meal of the smaller trout.

One unique aspect of the Wind River is the obvious history of previous human habitation—and not only American Indians, who obviously lived in and used this area for thousands of years. First, on the lower end of the trail, there are a number of plum trees that bear fruit and, in late summer, provide a great little snack to hikers heading up into the wilderness. Second, there are a few headstones and wooden grave markers in a clearing not too far from the river's confluence with the Salmon. One of the grave markers is for a man named Charlie White, who died in 1919—he was reportedly killed by Neil McMeekin.

Delaney Hunt shows off a Wind River redband rainbow trout while her brother, Cameron, looks on.

Following is the May 16, 1919 report from the *Idaho Post*:

> *Charles White was shot and killed by Neil McMeekin at Wind River, about 20 miles from Riggins, beyond Grangeville several days ago. White had sold his ranch to McMeekin, and the men had gone to the ranch from Grangeville for the purpose of making the transfer. It is said they quarreled about the personal property and that White attacked McMeekin with a pick when McMeekin shot White, killing him instantly. It took two days of hard riding on horseback and by stage for McMeekin to reach Grangeville where he gave himself up. He had notified the sheriff by telephone, and the sheriff and coroner met him on the road. McMeekin proceeded on to Grangeville and surrendered to the sheriff's office while the sheriff and coroner proceeded to the scene of the shooting.*

The Wind is like a lot of small tributaries to the Salmon in terms of the fish it holds and the opportunities it presents. The fact that it's a wilderness stream means it enjoys significant protection from development or extraction. With any luck at all, it'll be just like it is now when my kids are old enough to take their own children into the Gospel Hump to chase the Wind River's wild trout.

Flies

This won't surprise you if you've read through the book thus far—attractor dry flies are the obvious choice, at least when you start fishing the Wind. You'll probably want to try small streamers toward the confluence with the Salmon, where you're likely to latch into larger redbands and cutthroats, and perhaps a true trophy bull trout. During later summer, even bull trout will come to the top after high-floating hopper patterns.

Gear

A tenkara rod would be an ideal implement to use on the Wind River, particularly if you're more interested in catching fish on dry flies. The long, supple rods allow the angler to present dry flies perfectly in water like the Wind, which boasts conflicting currents and short runs with a short window of opportunity for the ideal drift. Anglers hoping to latch into the bigger redbands, cutthroats and perhaps a nice bull trout might want to consider conventional fly gear—a five-weight for streamers would be ideal, but you might be able to get by with a four-weight for casting dries and swinging small streamers in the longer runs.

Location

The Wind River is a tributary of the Salmon River located about twenty miles east of Riggins. More details can be found on page fifty-one of DeLorme's *Idaho Atlas & Gazetteer*.

Chapter 6

NORTHERN IDAHO

When the Lewis and Clark Expedition climbed into the mountains of western Montana in 1805, they knew they were in for a difficult challenge along the Lolo Trail. Even though it was only mid-September, the weather was turning ugly when they started into the Bitterroots. The party had stocked up on horses and supplies, thanks to the Lemhi Shoshones and a band of Flathead Indians they met in the Bitterroot Valley, but perhaps the most difficult portion of their journey west was at hand.

Eleven days later, and three horses light (the expedition was forced to slaughter and eat them), the Corps of Discovery emerged from the Lolo Trail at the Nez Perce Indian settlement of Weippe (pronounced Wee-Ipe). The group documented their harrowing experience along the trail. At one point, in his journal, William Clark wrote about being as cold and wet as he could ever remember—he even thought his feet would freeze in the leather moccasins he'd been given by the Indians.

They made contact with the Nez Perce Indians and made camp with them. With help, they hollowed out a handful of dugout canoes. Less than two months later, after shoving off into the Clearwater River, the party arrived at the mouth of the Columbia and the Pacific Ocean.

While the Lewis and Clark Expedition is perhaps what makes today's Lolo Pass famous, it's also important to note that about seventy years later, it was the escape route used by Chief Joseph and his Idaho band of Nez Perce Indians who refused to submit to U.S. government authority. Joseph and his band topped Lolo Pass and continued on the Lolo Trail to the upper reaches of the Big Hole River—on August 9, 1877, the U.S. Army and a handful of volunteers descended on the sleeping camp of Indians. A day later, ninety Nez Perce Indians and thirty-one soldiers and volunteers lay dead.

From a fishing standpoint, northern Idaho is defined by the Clearwater River drainage. The Clearwater itself is a legendary steelhead river, even today, with all the impediments facing Idaho's oceangoing rainbow trout. But all the rivers and streams that come together to form the Clearwater have a fishy legacy that rivals that of any system in the state.

Most of the waters that come together to form the Clearwater River start in the Bitterroot Mountains along Idaho's border with Montana. The South Fork of the Clearwater, which heads near the village of Elk City, is a terrific steelhead river in the fall and spring and runs through some of the prettiest big-tree country in the Northwest.

The Selway also gets runs of steelhead and salmon, but it's an underrated dry-fly trout stream as westslope cutthroats range up and down the river. One of my best dry-fly days ever was on a quick detour up the Selway in March one year while I was traveling to Lewiston for a meeting. I stumbled upon a prolific early season caddis hatch. It was the first time I'd ever been to the area, and I was just poking around, exploring…following the blue lines on my map. I rounded a bend on the road following the lower Selway and noticed some pretty big noses gulping beneath a swarm of blonde caddis flies.

I pulled the truck over, hopped out and assembled a five-weight as quickly as I could. Minutes later, I was standing on a rock in a little

Horses chauffeur eager anglers into the Kelly Creek backcountry of northern Idaho.

A westslope cutthroat trout falls for a hopper pattern in northern Idaho's fabled Kelly Creek.

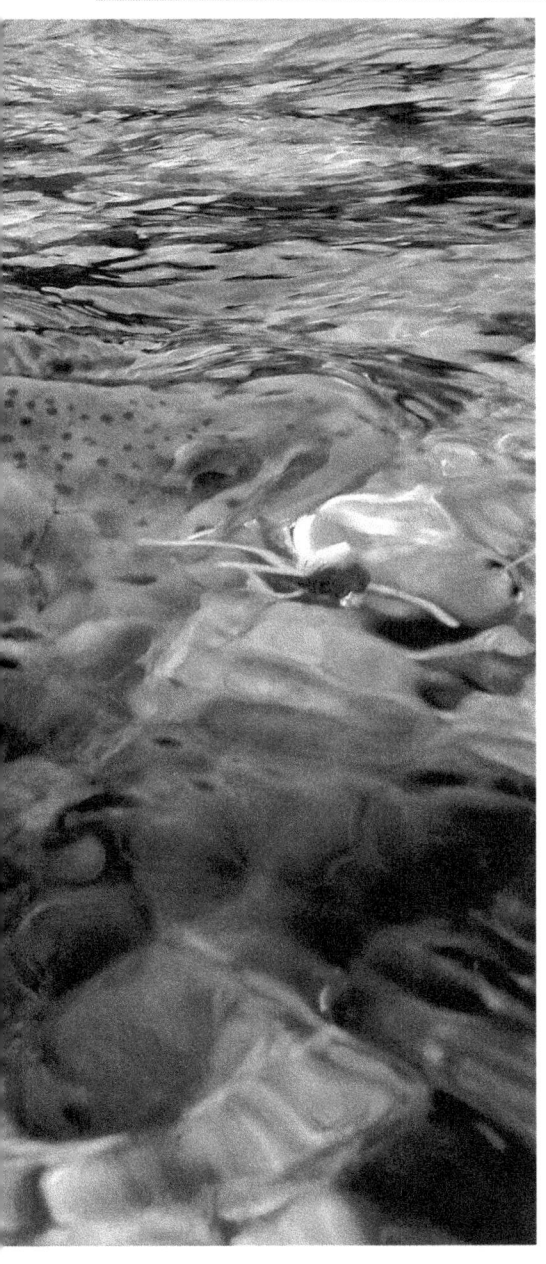

backwater slough of the river casting a size-fourteen Elk-hair caddis to rising cutthroats.

Farther north, the hallowed waters of Kelly Creek drain into the North Fork of the Clearwater—this might be the best westslope cutthroat trout fishery in the West. Still to the north, famous rivers like the St. Joe, the St. Maries and the Coeur d'Alene all eventually end up flowing into the Spokane River via Coeur d'Alene Lake. Hundreds of fishy little creeks web across the timbered landscape of northern Idaho—its climate is almost maritime, thanks to its lower elevation, but its waters are no less impressive. In southern and eastern Idaho, lodgepoles and aspens make up the timbered offerings, while here in the north, the timber consists of moss-laden fir, cedar, hemlock and huge spruce trees. Northern Idaho makes up the southern reaches of an inland temperate rainforest that extends northwest into Montana and north into British Columbia.

Johns Creek

Flowing north off the Clearwater Mountains into the South Fork of the Clearwater, Johns Creek may one day be the next officially designated Wild and Scenic river in Idaho.

If we're lucky. Or so I'm told. I've never actually fished it.

A few years back, Eric Barker, the outdoor and environmental reporter for the *Lewiston Tribune*, joined me, and we hiked the trail high above Johns Creek in hopes of fishing the stream with tenkara rods. Unfortunately, it was early June, and the area had received its share of rain and late spring snow, transforming the creek into a raging torrent.

But Eric and I—all wader-ed up and ready to fish for the redbands, westslope cutthroats and bull trout rumored to swim the pools and plunges of Johns Creek—hiked in nonetheless. We ventured a good four or five miles into the backcountry, taking in the scenery in this amazing landscape. We stepped over piles of wolf scat and marveled at the size of the footprints the big canines left behind. We spotted lots of whitetail deer sign and elk sign and stepped over little trickles of rainwater that would eventually end up in Johns Creek several hundred feet down a steep grade.

We had lunch under a stand of spruce, hot and sweaty in our waders and a bit trail-weary in our wading boots. Following the trail on the maps we had available, it looked like we would eventually rendezvous with the creek, but it wasn't meant to be. We finally gave in and wandered back to our rigs, parked in a pullout along the South Fork of the Clearwater. There, we opened a couple of beers and smiled at our luck.

It might sound like a bad day, but I think both of us took heart in the fact that the place we visited is being considered by a collaboration of user groups in northern Idaho for official Wild and Scenic designation. The designation would do a lot to protect the Johns Creek watershed—and selfishly, I know it'll be there, ready to fish, when I find my way back to the neighborhood.

Fortunately, Johns Creek is a lot like a host of other streams in the Clearwater Basin. I suppose that's what makes folks pay attention to them. Intact watersheds are harder and harder to come by, and the recognition of the importance they play in the general health of the forest is significant. Couple that with the fact that waters like Johns Creek could one day—like they no doubt were before the Lower Snake River dams were erected—serve as spawning and rearing habitat for large runs of chinook salmon and steelhead. I'm certain some anadromous fish find their way into Johns Creek—I've seen massive "B-run" steelhead staging and spawning in the South Fork of the Clearwater within a mile of the Johns Creek mouth.

It's likely that hatcheries alone—which are believed by many in Idaho to keep salmon and steelhead on life support—couldn't maintain Idaho's anadromous fish runs. Instead, it's probably the waters like Johns Creek or the nearby Twentymile Creek and Peasley Creek that keep the integrity of these rare and priceless fish somewhat intact.

I realize it sounds preachy and likely repetitive, but until we take some truly bold steps when it comes to dam removal and fish passage on the Lower Snake, Idaho will continue to have wonderful salmon and steelhead habitat but precious few salmon and steelhead.

If you ever get the chance to do more than just hike the trail into the Johns Creek backcountry, let me know. I'd love to know if the rumors are true and that redbands, westslopes and bull trout swim in its waters. But you better do it soon—I intend to beat you to it.

Flies

No, I haven't fished Johns Creek, but I'd wager that my usual assortment of summertime attractor dry flies would work just fine in its clear waters. I'd likely start with something simple, like an Adams, hoping the stream's resident rainbows and cutthroats would come to the surface. I'd chase larger fish by stripping black and olive Woolly Buggers through the longer, deeper runs. Later in the year, I'd go with hopper and beetle patterns.

Gear

When Eric and I walked in, it was June, and the creek was swollen with rain and snow runoff. It's a sizeable tributary to the South Fork, and I might consider waders any day of the year. Assuming it's geologically similar to the Clearwater, I'd encourage some stout wading boots and maybe some steel studs rather than just felt. Of course, in high summer, when it's good and hot, I'd be tempted to wade Johns Creek wet.

Location

Johns Creek is a tributary of the South Fork of the Clearwater River. It can be found on page fifty-five of DeLorme's *Idaho Atlas & Gazetteer*.

THE PACK RIVER

In far northern Idaho, running south almost from the Canadian border, the Pack River forms and runs through the Kaniksu National Forest and a host of Idaho state lands into a corner arm of Lake Pend Oreille. This is the boundary country, where the last of Idaho's endangered woodland caribou ghost in and out of the timber. There are somewhere in the neighborhood of forty of these large ungulates left in far northern Idaho—that's about the same estimate as the number of endangered grizzly bears that live south of the border in the Selkirk Mountains of Idaho and northeast Washington State.

The Pack River in the Idaho Panhandle is a pristine creek in its headwaters, but in lower elevations, it's in need of restoration.

Another endangered critter inhabits the Pack River drainage: Idaho's native char, the bull trout.

I know this because a few years back, I drove the Upper Pack River Road, stopping and casting flies to small westslope cutthroats, wondering if a predatory char that I'd been warned about on the signs posted along the river would slip out of the depths and crush one of the diminutive trout.

While I've seen this happen in a few places in Idaho, I didn't see it happen on the Pack River. There are a few reasons for this, not the least of which is the health of the watershed, particularly in the lower third or so.

The Pack slices north to south, draining a significant portion of the Idaho panhandle, and its upper reaches are shrouded by tall spruce, hemlock and cedar trees. It's a temperate rainforest stream that's quite austere in the upper reaches and, sadly, a bit impaired the closer it gets to Lake Pend Oreille, thanks to agricultural runoff and sediment from past mining and logging activity.

Additionally, the Pack River is part of a drainage that has some invasive species issues. In Lake Pend Oreille, lake trout, a nonnative char native to the Great Lakes, is taking a toll on kokanee salmon, cutthroat trout and, yes, native bull trout. The bull trout once migrated out of the lake and into its tributaries—they still do in smaller numbers. But the largest migratory bull trout population once migrated into the Pend Oreille River, downstream from Lake Pend Oreille. However, in 1952, the Albeni Falls Dam was constructed just upstream of the Idaho-Washington border, and that was the death knell for that run of bull trout.

I realize that's a lengthy explanation for why fishing in the Pack River may not be as good as it could be. I also realize I'm likely not inspiring many readers to wander up the Upper Pack River Road to chase small resident cutthroat trout. That's intentional, of course. It's a reminder that without intact habitat, angling opportunity suffers.

Efforts are underway to remove lake trout from Lake Pend Oreille—commercial-grade netting operations are in place, and the Idaho Department of Fish and Game has put a fifteen-dollar bounty on all lake trout caught by anglers from the lake.

About a decade ago, the Pack River Watershed Council was formed to address the sediment and nutrient pollution in the lower river. Perhaps, with collaboration and compromise, enough progress can be made to return both the lake's fishery to a better balance and the lower Pack River to a healthier state. Then maybe the native bull trout will once again be able to migrate into the upper Pack River—along with migratory cutthroat trout and kokanee salmon—and chase those resident westslope cutthroats like they're supposed to.

The little cutthroats I hooked that day, though, seemed to get the most out of what the upper river does offer. I suppose there could be solace, at least for the smaller resident fish, in the fact that there appear to be precious few migratory fish in the upper river to eat them. But for anglers, the health of the system directly impacts opportunity, from the top of the system to the bottom.

Here's hoping the efforts to improve the Pend Oreille watershed are successful. Perhaps tomorrow's anglers will enjoy a healthier Pack River and the opportunity to chase big fish in the beautiful upper reaches of this idyllic Idaho stream.

Flies

Predictably, I used attractor dry flies that day on the Pack River, and while the cutthroats were plentiful and beautiful, they weren't very big. If I were to fish it again, I'd go a little smaller—size sixteen to eighteen Humpies and Adams would be among my first choices. Later in the year, I'd use smaller terrestrials, like ants or beetles.

Gear

Go light on the upper Pack—try a three-weight or four-weight rod. Or consider using a tenkara rod, as the long, willowy rod would allow for ideal placement of dry flies, particularly in runs with competing currents and varied water depth. As for waders, the Pack is big enough to justify them, and it's plenty cold in the upper reaches.

Location

The Pack River flows from north to south into Lake Pend Oreille. It can be found on page sixty-two of DeLorme's *Idaho Atlas & Gazetteer*.

Cayuse Creek

A few minutes spent studying a map of north-central Idaho is all it takes to realize the havoc wreaked on the region's oceangoing fish the day Dworshak Dam blocked passage of salmon and steelhead into the upper reaches of the North Fork of the Clearwater River. The dam is the tallest straight-axis dam in North America—there is no fish passage around it.

It first blocked the river in the name of flood control in 1973, and a year later, the powerhouse became operational. The runs of chinook salmon and big "B-run" steelhead that once cruised up the North Fork were history. The dam cost $312 million when it was constructed. In

A Cayuse Creek cutthroat trout.

the name of mitigation, the Dworshak National Fish Hatchery was constructed downstream of the dam. It cost $21 million.

I would wager that, over the long term, the cost of losing the North Fork's anadromous fish has far exceeded the value of the dam when it comes to power production and flood control. Today, the dam produces only half the power it was designed to produce, simply because producing full power would create such a flow into the river below the dam that a second dam would be needed to contain it.

It's one of the great ironic tragedies in the Northwest when it comes to managing our oceangoing fish—and, sadly, there are many.

If there's a silver lining to this particular tragic story, it's that, for fly fishers, the fishing for native westslope cutthroat trout in the North Fork and its tributaries is probably the best in the state and maybe the West.

There's some big country locked away behind Dworshak Reservoir, and it would take years to explore it all with a fly rod. The North Fork is a massive drainage, containing some of the best-known wild trout waters on earth. The river itself, particularly in its upper reaches, is a fantastic fishery for native westslope cutthroat trout, a few rainbows and the occasional bull trout. And most anglers have Kelly Creek on their bucket list—something about twenty-inch native cutthroat trout rising to dry flies makes us all willing to venture miles off the pavement to fish.

And if there are secrets to be unlocked in this drainage—and because it's so remote, I believe that there are many—Cayuse Creek is easily among the best. The stream, which joins Kelly Creek in a backcountry confluence in the shadow of the Bitterroots, flows deep and green and courses with native westslope cutthroats and rangy bull trout. It takes some effort to get to Cayuse Creek, but it's worthwhile.

The westslope cutthroats in the North Fork country are, for some reason, a bit more aggressive than cutthroats I've coaxed to the fly elsewhere. In Cayuse Creek, they tend to occupy the longer, deeper runs, and since they don't see too many flies over the course of a year, they're pretty naïve—if you can find a lively run, it's possible to pull three or four nice-sized fish from it before the rest of the cutties get wise.

The size of the average cutthroat in Cayuse Creek is similar to that of an average fish caught in Kelly Creek—probably in the twelve- to thirteen-inch range. But much larger cutthroats are occasionally found in this stream, and I've been the grateful beneficiary of their zest to hit a fly. On my last visit, I was lucky enough to bring a couple of fish to hand in the twenty-inch range. Once, while fighting a decent cutthroat, a truly large bull trout ghosted up from the depths to see if it could make a meal out of the struggling fish at the end of my leader. Thankfully—for the cutthroat, at least—the bull trout decided against taking a bite out of it.

Northern Idaho

A Kelly Creek cutthroat trout. *Photo by Greg McReynolds.*

While the fishing in Cayuse Creek is truly incredible, the real magic occurs when you lift your head from the water and take a look around. This might be the best of Idaho—roadless, wild and largely intact (it's tough to forget that these streams might be coursing with salmon and steelhead in a perfect world). Timbered with spruce, fir and cedars, this evergreen landscape is lush and productive.

Trickles of water start from snowmelt high on the western slope of the Bitterroots and combine to form crystal-clear, cold mountain streams. They come together with the peaks in the background to create some of the most scenic and idyllic mountain watersheds even the most imaginative fly fisher can conjure up.

A wildfire burns along the banks of northern Idaho's Lochsa River.

There might not be a better place to be on a bluebird summer day than miles away from the road on the banks of Cayuse Creek. For an avid backcountry fly fisher, there's no doubt.

The hike up Cayuse from the roadless confluence with Kelly Creek is absolutely stunning, and you'll likely share the trail with horse packers heading into the backcountry to fish or, later in the year, hunt elk. The Clearwater elk herd is down of late—the reintroduction of wolves into the area in 1995, coupled with some habitat issues due to overgrowth (there hasn't been a significant fire in the area since the Great Burn of the early 1900s), have led to some challenges for hunters. There are fewer clearings that elk need to succeed, and that makes them vulnerable to predation. A balance will eventually work itself out, but it will require patience and compromise from both sportsmen and the environmental community. And frankly, a good fire or two, within reason, would do the area some good.

Thankfully, a collaborative group of interested forest users assembled by Senator Mike Crapo is examining how to best protect the Clearwater region well into the future, both for responsible extractive use, like mining and logging, and for recreational use, which today is a very significant economic driver in the region.

Here's hoping that long after this writing, the North Fork country is still an amazing fishery and that others who value this landscape can find ways to manage it appropriately, with coming generations in mind. Today, it's perhaps Idaho's shiniest crown jewel. It would be a shame to lose it, don't you think?

Flies

The cutthroats in Cayuse Creek always seem to be looking up—an angler should start with a well-presented dry fly and keep a few extras handy because, if your day goes well, you'll be wearing thin the usual Adams, Stimulators, caddis patterns and Humpies. Later in the summer, foam ant and beetle patterns, or even small hoppers (size twelve or so) will bring big cutties to the top, and "hopper-dropper" rigs featuring a high-floating Chernobyl Ant over a size-ten Girdle Bug can prove very effective. The creek's cutthroats will hit streamers, too, as will the bull trout that call Cayuse home. Remember, fishing for endangered bull trout is catch-and-release only (and it's probably not a bad idea to approach all of your Cayuse Creek fishing with this philosophy in mind).

Gear

Cayuse Creek isn't a huge backcountry stream, and you might be tempted to go light where fly tackle is concerned. I'd advise against it—go with a tried-and-true five-weight rod with floating line and stick with 3X tippet, just to avoid overplaying the priceless native fish in the emerald-green waters of this cherished stream. Also, if you're using streamers for the cutthroats and bull trout, you'll likely need the added backbone of the larger rod. Early in the year, Cayuse Creek carries a heavy load of snowmelt, so I'd recommend waders if you can carry them with you into the backcountry. Later in the year, it can get warm in the Clearwater country, so wet wading is perfectly fine. I'd still recommend wading boots, though, as the creek bottom can be a bit tricky and good footing is important.

Location

Cayuse Creek is a tributary to the world-famous Kelly Creek in the North Fork of the Clearwater drainage. You find specific access instructions on page sixty-three of DeLorme's *Idaho Atlas & Gazetteer*.

ABOUT THE AUTHOR

*C*hris Hunt is the national communications director for Trout Unlimited and a freelance writer and author who lives in Idaho Falls. He's called Idaho home for fifteen years, and while his work and his writing take him all over the country and all over the world, he's most at home when he's on a single-track trail deep in the Idaho backcountry, equipped with a can of bear spray and supple three-weight fly rod.

Chris is a former award-winning journalist—he won the 2004 Dolly Connelly Award for Excellence in Environmental Journalism for a series of articles he wrote for the *Idaho State Journal* on cutthroat trout in the West—and the father of two fly-fishing children, Delaney and Cameron. He blogs frequently at tu.org and eatmorebrooktrout.com and is a frequent contributor to MidCurrent.com and *Hatch* magazine, as well as a host of other fly-fishing magazines.

Visit us at
www.historypress.net

This title is also available as an e-book

www.ingramcontent.com/pod-product-compliance
Lightning Source LLC
Chambersburg PA
CBHW042143160426
43201CB00022B/2395